THE MARITIME INFRASTRUCTURE RECOVERY PLAN

FOR
THE NATIONAL STRATEGY FOR MARITIME SECURITY

APRIL 2006

FOREWORD

By signing National Security Presidential Directive 41/Homeland Security Presidential Directive 13 (NSPD 41/HSPD 13), President Bush underscored the importance of securing the Maritime Domain, defined as *"All areas and things of, on, under, relating to, adjacent to, or bordering on a sea, ocean, or other navigable waterway, including all maritime-related activities, infrastructure, people, cargo, and vessels and other conveyances."*

NSPD 41/HSPD 13 established a Maritime Security Policy Coordinating Committee (MSPCC)—the first coordinating committee specifically tasked to address this issue—to oversee the development of a National Strategy for Maritime Security (NSMS) and eight supporting implementation plans:

- The **National Plan to Achieve Maritime Domain Awareness** lays the foundation for an effective understanding of anything associated with the Maritime Domain and identifying threats as early and as distant from our shores as possible.
- The **Global Maritime Intelligence Integration Plan** uses existing capabilities to integrate all available intelligence regarding potential threats to U.S. interests in the Maritime Domain.
- The **Maritime Operational Threat Response Plan** aims for coordinated U.S. government response to threats against the U.S. and its interests in the Maritime Domain by establishing roles and responsibilities, which enable the government to respond quickly and decisively.
- The **International Outreach Strategy to Enhance Maritime Security** provides a framework to coordinate all maritime security initiatives undertaken with foreign governments and international organizations, and solicits international support for enhanced maritime security.
- The **Maritime Infrastructure Recovery Plan** recommends standardized procedures for restoration of maritime transportation systems following an incident of national significance.
- The **Maritime Transportation Systems Security Plan** provides strategic recommendations to holistically improve the security of maritime transportation systems.
- The **Maritime Commerce Security Plan** establishes a comprehensive plan to secure the maritime supply chain.
- The **Domestic Outreach Plan** engages non-federal input to assist with the development and implementation of maritime security policies resulting from NSPD 41/HSPD 13.

Although these plans address different aspects of maritime security, they are mutually linked and reinforce each other. Together, NSMS and its supporting plans represent the beginning of a comprehensive national effort to promote global economic stability and protect legitimate activities, while preventing hostile or illegal acts within the Maritime Domain.

TABLE OF CONTENTS

I. INTRODUCTION TO THE MARITIME INFRASTRUCTURE RECOVERY PLAN

"A nation as vital and thriving as ours cannot become hermetically sealed. Even less can we afford to be overwhelmed by fear or paralyzed by the existence of threats. That's why we need to adopt a risk-based approach in both our operations and our philosophy. Risk management is fundamental to managing the threat, while retaining our quality of life and living in freedom. Risk management must guide our decision-making as we examine how we can best organize to prevent, respond and recover from an attack.... We all live with a certain amount of risk. That means that we tolerate that something bad can happen; we adjust our lives based on probability; and we take reasonable precautions."

> DHS Secretary Chertoff
> George Washington University
> March 16, 2005

In addition to being an integral part of the HSPD-13 plans, the strategic guidance in the MIRP is reflected in the provisions of the National Maritime Security Plan (NMSP). The NMSP is a Maritime Transportation Security Act (MTSA) plan that addresses the restoration of domestic cargo flow following a security incident that occurs under, in, on, or adjacent to waters subject to the jurisdiction of the United States.

The Maritime Infrastructure Recovery Plan, the Maritime Commerce Security Plan, and the Maritime Transportation System Security Plan were developed in close coordination under the National Strategy for Maritime Security. The Maritime Commerce Security Plan contains recommendations to promote international maritime supply chain security and the Maritime Transportation System Security Plan addresses security of the Maritime Transportation System (MTS) as a system, including vessels, facilities, and ports. Both support the recovery of maritime capabilities.

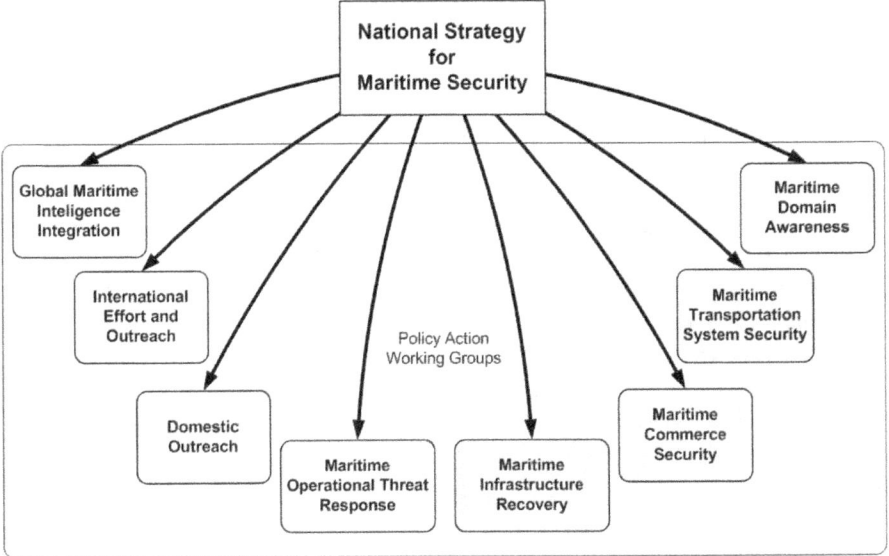

Figure 1.1 National Strategy for Maritime Security Policy Action Working Groups

The MIRP contains procedures for recovery management and provides mechanisms for national, regional, and local decision-makers to set priorities for redirecting commerce, a primary means of restoring domestic cargo flow. This plan is employed when the Secretary of Homeland Security declares an actual or threatened Transportation Security Incident (TSI; 33 CFR 101.105) that occurs under, in, on, or adjacent to waters subject to the jurisdiction of the United States, to be an Incident of National Significance (INS), in accordance with the criteria set out in the National Response Plan (NRP) and HSPD-5. Any such TSI declared to be an INS accordingly is referred to as a "national TSI."

Additionally, the MIRP reflects the organizational constructs detailed in the NRP, as well as the use of Incident Command System (ICS) and unified command procedures. As such, the plan can be used for other similarly disruptive incidents requiring maritime infrastructure recovery management.

Following an incident that triggers the implementation of this plan, the MIRP is used to guide the designees of the Secretary of Homeland Security in the decision making process to maintain the nation's MTS operational capabilities, and if compromised, to restore transportation capabilities.

In recognizing that recovery management takes place at several levels (i.e., national, regional, and local), the MIRP describes recovery management considerations for the incident site, non-incident support sites, as well as the national system-wide MTS. Decision-making affecting the nation's entire MTS draws on both domestic and international resources for recovery. The operational decisions to facilitate the diversion of cargo to alternate sites, including foreign ports, will be based on just-in-time information; currently there is no recognized methodology or uniform standards for measuring either domestic or foreign port cargo-handling capacity. Information of this type is necessary to support recovery efforts; however, it is not currently available. The need for port cargo-handling reserve capacity information is addressed in the Next Steps/ Recommendations Section of this plan.

Coincidental to operational considerations in recovery are those issues associated with the security posture necessary to re-establish any affected port to pre-incident equilibrium. Security postures are based on measured, targeted responses to ensure the public's well being and minimize disruption to the continuity of commerce. A basic assumption of the plan is that the MTS should not shut down as an automatic response to a maritime security incident.

Since this plan focuses on maritime transportation capabilities as a system, it only addresses the restoration of individual physical assets to restore the MTS. The vast majority of maritime transportation infrastructure assets are privately owned and operated. The decision to repair, replace, or rebuild private physical assets is a private sector decision. However, the federal government acknowledges that federal assistance may be required to help private industry in restoring critical cargo-handling infrastructure. Additionally, the plan recognizes that further study is needed to determine how the federal government can provide assistance or create incentives to private maritime stakeholders to establish sufficient critical cargo-handling infrastructure. (See Next Steps/Recommendations Section).

Since the MIRP provides recovery management procedures for decision makers at various levels, the procedures are general in nature to provide flexibility for recovery management. With over 2,100 possible threat scenarios in hundreds of ports, the variables affecting MTS recovery are too myriad to provide detailed procedures. Nevertheless, the procedures place emphasis on the importance of intelligence gathering and the use of risk management principles to make the decision-making considerations pertinent to any security-incident scenario. While the use of one particular risk-management model is not advocated, the plan strongly recommends that the recovery decision-making process involve personnel who have been trained in risk management/analysis so as to avoid uninformed decisions that would impose unnecessary constraints on the MTS. (See Next Steps/Recommendation Section about the need for risk management expertise.) The management of risk is also recognized in the Maritime Commerce Security Plan as being essential to balancing security with the desire to maintain the free flow of commerce. The Maritime Transportation System Security Plan recommends improvement of MTS security through the development of risk assessment methodologies. (See Appendix B for a description of Risk Management Principles).

In recognition that the federal government must work with private maritime stakeholders to restore passenger and cargo flow in an efficient manner, the plan encourages planning for recovery through development of private sector contingency/continuity of operations plans. The private sector is encouraged to develop recovery operations plans (within their business contingency plans) that include diversion of vessels to alternate ports and to engage in voluntary exchange of information with other companies to avoid conflicts in the use of alternate ports. (See the Roles and Responsibilities Section for the Private Sector).

The 9/11 Commission's report suggests the need for standards for private sector emergency preparedness and business continuity. In light of that identified need, this plan acknowledges that the federal government and the maritime private sector stakeholders should work together to plan for all aspects of recovery of the MTS after a security incident. The private sector is encouraged to collaborate with government and other stakeholders using professional organizations and Area Maritime Security (AMS) Committees. The Maritime Transportation System Security Plan suggests leveraging the value of AMS Committees by establishing threat response and recovery subcommittees and developing communications vehicles for use during normal and threat response/ recovery modes. There are many opportunities for communication and information sharing between government and the private sector; however, the MIRP recommends expanding the access to, and the capabilities of, one particular network in dealing with recovery activities (i.e. the Homeland Security Information Network (HSIN). (See Section IV – Concept of Operations as well as Next Steps/Recommendations about the communications network).

PURPOSE

The purpose of the MIRP is to establish a comprehensive approach to recover from a national TSI. As stated in the introductory portion of the plan, the focus of this plan is on maritime transportation capabilities (i.e., restoration of passenger and cargo flow) and minimizing impact of a security incident on the U.S. economy.

Assuming the effect of a national TSI (or other similarly disruptive incident) impairs the loading/offloading or movement of vessels, this plan provides a framework with clearly defined roles to facilitate restoration of cargo flow, as well as passenger vessel activity. Restoration of cargo flow and passenger vessel activity may include the redirecting/diverting of vessels to ports with reserve or excess capacity.

To assist with the recovery/restoration of maritime transportation capabilities, the MIRP accomplishes or considers the following:

- Provides recovery management procedures for the Secretary of Homeland Security and designated representatives (e.g., the Interagency Incident Management Group (IIMG)) to make decisions affecting national maritime recovery efforts;
- Provides recovery management procedures for those making decisions at the incident site and at non-incident sites that provide support;
- Recognizes that, based on the nature and circumstances of the incident, a transition in focus from homeland defense operations to recovery management may occur between the Secretary of Defense and the Secretary of Homeland Security[1];
- Takes into consideration initial post-incident decisions made by senior officials from the U.S. Coast Guard (USCG) and the U.S. Customs and Border Protection (CBP) regarding short-term, targeted operational actions to help maintain flow of commerce through non-incident sites ;
- Lists roles and responsibilities of federal, state, local, tribal governments, and the private sector. The listing is specific to the functional responsibilities related to recovery of maritime transportation capabilities;
- To evaluate the effectiveness of the plan, the MIRP subscribes to an exercise program that includes periodic validation of the concepts of this recovery plan; and
- Identifies next steps and makes recommendations to improve recovery management.

OBJECTIVE

The primary objective of the MIRP is to provide guidance for federal decision makers to use in restoring maritime transportation capabilities if compromised, specifically the restoration of cargo flow and passenger vessel activity after a national TSI. This guidance includes recommended recovery management procedures to assist in the development of viable strategies or Courses of Action (COA).

To meet the primary objective stated above, a federal inter-agency working group was convened to develop a plan to satisfy the following functional planning objectives:

---

[1] During and following any homeland defense operations event, the Secretary of the Department of Homeland Security retains the lead for maritime infrastructure recovery management, and will ensure such activities align with homeland defense operations. Nothing in this plan will be construed to take precedence over homeland defense operations, including assignment of U.S. Coast Guard forces in accordance with current directives.

- Identify pre-designated key national government/industry stakeholders immediately available to advise the Secretary of Homeland Security on matters pertaining to recovery from INS affecting the Maritime Domain;
- Recommend national priorities for recovery of maritime transportation systems after a national TSI:
  - Define the criteria for identifying maritime critical infrastructure (MCI) across various maritime transportation subsystems;
  - Use Customs and Border Protection (CBP) inspection criteria for screening cargo to assist maritime recovery efforts and manage risk;
- Recommend federal policies and procedures for recovery of national maritime transportation after a security incident (and support recovery of critical local and regional transportation systems);
  - Establish standard procedures for setting decision-making priorities for recovery nationally, and for supporting recovery of critical local and regional transportation systems;
  - Set standard procedures for integrating national recovery priorities with national military requirements;
  - Maintain consistency with the National Response Plan (NRP);
  - Conduct a review of all legal authorities to ensure effective federal coordination of recovery and identify any recommend changes to eliminate statutory and regulatory gaps;
  - Establish standard procedures for assessing recovery requirements and developing potential recovery options within the Maritime Transportation System (MTS);
- Describe a maritime infrastructure recovery exercise program consistent with the National Exercise Program; and
- Specify procedures for coordinating among federal, state, local and private sector partners, and cooperation with foreign governments and international entities, as appropriate.

APPLICABILITY

Prior to declaration by the Secretary of Homeland Security that a TSI is an INS, response and recovery efforts are conducted under the purview and authority of Area Maritime Security (AMS) Plans in force for the affected geographic area, or Area of Responsibility (AOR), in which an incident has taken place.

When the Secretary of Homeland Security declares the TSI to be an Incident of National Significance ("national TSI"), decision-makers at the national level, as well as other levels, will address implications to the maritime industry nationwide, and will provide oversight to local and regional recovery operations utilizing the MIRP in conjunction with the National Maritime Security Plan (NMSP). The shift from local and regional to national incident management involves the activation of many plans. See the diagram in Section IV. Concept of Operations, for a graphic representation of the relationship of these plans.

AUTHORITIES

Various federal statutory authorities and policies provide the basis for federal actions and activities in the context of maritime infrastructure recovery. As described in the Foreword of this plan, the MIRP uses the foundation provided by the National Strategy for Maritime Security (NSMS) pursuant to the National Security Presidential Directive - 41/Homeland Security Presidential Directive - 13 (NSPD-41/HSPD-13) in conjunction with the National Maritime Security Plan to provide guidance for the restoration and recovery of cargo flow.

The MIRP does not in any way alter the existing authorities of individual federal departments and agencies. The MIRP does not convey new authorities upon the Secretary of Homeland Security or any other federal official. Rather, this plan establishes the coordinating structures, processes and protocols required to integrate specific statutory and policy authorities of various federal departments and agencies in a collective framework for action and activities to recover from a national TSI. All questions concerning specific authority and jurisdiction must be referred to competent counsel.

FEDERALISM

In regard to authority to preempt state action, when a Coast Guard official takes action pursuant to this plan, and that action implements or enforces an existing federal legal requirement for maritime security, it would be inconsistent with the Federalism principles set out in the Executive Order 13132 to construe that action as not preempting state laws or regulations that conflict with the existing federal legal requirement. This is because owners or operators of facilities or vessels, including those owned and operated by states, that may be subject to federal legal requirements for maritime security for both performance and operating standards, must have one uniform national standard that they must meet. Vessels and shipping companies, particularly, would be confronted with an unreasonable burden if they had to comply with varying requirements as they moved from state to state. Therefore, the Federalism principles enumerated by the Supreme Court in U.S. v. Locke, 529 U.S. 89 (2000) regarding field preemption of certain state vessel safety, equipment, and operating requirements extends to actions taken pursuant to this plan which implement or enforce an existing federal legal requirement for maritime security, especially regarding the longstanding history of significant Coast Guard maritime security regulation and control of vessels for security purposes. The same considerations apply to facilities, at least insofar as a state law or regulation applicable to the same subject for the purpose of protecting the security of the facility would conflict with a federal legal requirement; in other words, it would either actually conflict or would frustrate an overriding federal need for uniformity.

Finally, it is important to note that actions taken by the Coast Guard pursuant to this plan which implement or enforce an existing federal legal requirement for maritime security bear on national and international commerce, where there is no constitutional presumption of concurrent State regulation. Many aspects of federal legal requirements for maritime security are based on the U.S. international treaty obligations regarding vessel and port facility security contained in the International Convention for the Safety or Life at Sea, 1974, TIAS 9700; Rectification (1982), TIAS 10626, as amended, and the complementary International Ship and Port Facility Security Code. These international obligations reinforce the need for uniformity regarding maritime commerce.

The authorities of federal agencies, other than the Coast Guard, may also preempt state action due a need to maintain national uniformity, to satisfy international obligations, to carry out express Congressional intent, to comply with specific case law, or due to a history of longstanding regulation. All questions concerning specific agency authority to preempt state action must be referred to competent counsel.

Notwithstanding the foregoing position, the federal government intends to consult with appropriate state officials and the private sector as set out in the plan.

DISCRETIONARY ENFORCEMENT

Following an incident that triggers the implementation of this plan, the MIRP anticipates that the private sector and appropriate federal government agencies will take actions that will result in large scale re-routing of vessel and cargo traffic. This re-routing will result in, among many other things, private sector requests for vessel, crew, and cargo clearances outside of normal lead times currently required by law. Further, re-routing of traffic and the need to move high priority cargo may result in the use of foreign registered platforms to carry cargo on coastwise voyages, and use of U.S. registered platforms to carry cargo on foreign voyages, or both, depending on the circumstances.

This plan does not change any authorities applicable to the aforementioned clearance processes or voyage routes. Federal agencies must be prepared to balance the continued need for security against the need to recover cargo flow to support the national economy. Accordingly, agencies should ease enforcement of laws regulating notices of arrival, crew and cargo manifests, and the coastwise trade, when such actions would enhance restoration of cargo flow without compromising security. Specifically, when re-routing of cargo results in changes only to destination and lead time of notice, and not to other required information such as cargo, vessel description and crew composition, agencies should be favorably disposed to approve such changes as soon as possible on an individual or company fleet-wide basis.

Agencies also must recognize that strict enforcement of coastwise trade regulations that results in a bar to employment of otherwise capable and secure platforms (U.S. or foreign registered) to move cargo to, from, or within the United States from foreign or domestic ports, may not be in the national interest. Accordingly, agencies should ease enforcement of coastwise trade regulations to ensure that all available platforms are readily available to move cargo to, from, or within the United States, from foreign or domestic ports, in the weeks following the incident, so that adverse economic impact is mitigated as soon as possible.

II. PLANNING ASSUMPTIONS AND CONSIDERATIONS

THE MARITIME INFRASTRUCTURE RECOVERY PLAN (MIRP) IS BASED ON THE FOLLOWING PLANNING ASSUMPTIONS AND CONSIDERATIONS:

- The MIRP is a guidance document used by incident managers, advisors, and decision makers;
- Implementation of the MIRP is based on the occurrence of a national TSI, which has been declared an INS by the Secretary of DHS, that has impaired or threatens to impair the loading/offloading or movement of vessels and disrupts the flow of commerce;
- This plan assumes that a national TSI has been declared, the National Response Plan (NRP), and its Interagency Incident Management Group (IIMG) has convened and is available to make national-level recommendations regarding the restoration of cargo flow and maritime infrastructure recovery;
- Recovery operations are based on risk management principles—100% security of the MTS cannot be guaranteed before or following an incident;
- The goals of decision makers utilizing the MIRP are:
  o Facilitate achieving the optimum balance between ports and waterways security and the recovery of maritime transportation capabilities,
  o Maximize the Maritime Transportation System's (MTS) continued operational equilibrium,
  o Minimize disruption to the U. S. economy from unnecessarily constrained cargo flow;
- Infrastructure refers to the Maritime Transportation System (MTS) and those facilities, structures, and assets vital to the Nation's ports (33 CFR 101.105);
- Use of the phrase "recovery or restoration of cargo flow" refers to recovery of goods, wares, and merchandise (33CFR 101.105) and restoration of maritime transportation capabilities in the MTS. Additionally, when referring to either recovery or restoration of cargo flow, the phrase includes recovery management associated with passenger vessel activity;
- The MIRP will be implemented with awareness of the initial measured and targeted response and recovery actions exercised by senior U.S. Coast Guard and Customs and Border Protection officials;
- A basic assumption of the plan is that the MTS should not be shut down as an automatic response to a maritime security incident;
- The plan includes next steps/recommendations to assess reserve or excess port-handling capacity at ports in North America (including both Canada and Mexico) and at other ports outside of North America. *The capacity of a port is the level at which the port can move cargo and passengers through the Maritime Transportation System, including the ability to safely and securely load and unload cargo and passengers and accommodate inter-modal operations*;
- "Minimizing damage (i.e., physical infrastructure damage) from attacks within the Maritime Domain" is covered under separate preparedness and incident response plans and, therefore, is not addressed in the MIRP;

- Key public and private maritime sector stakeholder inputs were considered in the development of the MIRP;
- Planners will consult with the private sector to update the MIRP to ensure meaningful, up-to-date decision-making information for federal officials; and
- Periodically, the MIRP will be updated as required to incorporate new Presidential Directives, legislative changes, and procedural changes based on lessons learned from exercises and actual events.

III. ROLES AND RESPONSIBILITIES

The Maritime Infrastructure Recovery Plan (MIRP) provides a list of *Functional Responsibilities*, as related to maritime transportation, that various agencies and private sector entities may perform to recover from a national TSI, which has been declared an INS. Decision makers at the incident site, the non-incident site, and the national levels may find this information useful in expanding their knowledge about recovery-specific responsibilities for federal, state, and local governments as well as the private sector. Descriptions of general roles and responsibilities of various organizations can be found in the National Response Plan (NRP).

FEDERAL GOVERNMENT – FUNCTIONAL RESPONSIBILITIES FOR RECOVERY

Functional responsibilities for the recovery of maritime transportation infrastructure systems are listed below for federal departments/agencies identified with recovery responsibilities:

Department of Homeland Security (DHS)

- Act as the Principal Federal Official (PFO) for domestic incident management.
- Coordinate federal maritime infrastructure recovery operations within the U.S.
- Coordinate federal government resources.

U.S. Coast Guard (USCG)

- Provide on-scene resources to assist in assessments;
- Act as the PFO when directed by the Secretary of DHS or as the Senior Federal Official (SFO);
- Participate in recovery planning by developing Area Maritime Security (AMS) Plans and collaborate with maritime stakeholders, especially local harbor safety committees;
- As the COTP/FMSC:
    - o Develop and implement AMS Plans;
    - o Control vessel traffic, movement and anchorage;
    - o Establish and enforce safety and security zones;
    - o Control access to and operations of facilities under, in, or adjacent to waters subject to the jurisdiction of the U.S.;
    - o Control the movement of vessels carrying Certain Dangerous Cargos (CDC);
- Furnish available personnel, equipment or other resource support as requested;
- Provide port security measures to reduce potential, future threats and to ensure integrity of the existing infrastructure system;
- Track Notice of Arrival (NOA) information from ships entering U.S waters and ensure changes to NOA are provided to the appropriate Coast Guard and Customs and Border Protection (CBP) officials at alternate ports of entry;
- As part of AMS Plans, in coordination with appropriate stakeholders and other government agencies, be aware of maximum vessel, cargo and inter-modal throughput within the respective area of responsibility;

- Consider temporary easement of enforcement of regulations to facilitate re-routing of cargo, including NOA lead times;
- Support CBP in the screening and evaluating of cargo movement into and out of the U.S.;
- In support of ESF #3 of the NRP, coordinate with the U.S Army Corps of Engineers (USACE) to mark and remove obstructions declared to be hazards to navigation;
- Ensure safety of navigation and security of AOR prior to reopening of any waterway;
- Assist in debris and contaminated debris management activities;
- Provide support as outlined in ESFs 1, 3, 4, 9, 10, 11, 13 of the National Response Plan (NRP) and any other tasking as directed by the Secretary of DHS.

U.S. Customs and Border Protection (CBP)

- Provide on-scene resources to assist in assessments;
- In coordination with appropriate stakeholders and other government agencies, be aware of maximum available vessel, cargo and inter-modal throughput within the respective area of responsibility;
- Screen and evaluate cargo, crew, and passenger movement into and out of the U.S;
- Conduct hands-on physical boardings of vessels with highest-risk cargo;
- Inspect and search vessels, conveyances, persons, and cargo within the Customs territory of the U.S.;
- Detain and seize vessels, cargo, and contraband;
- Authorize lading and unlading of cargo;
- Determine the admissibility of persons arriving in the U.S.;
- Collect, integrate and analyze maritime intelligence concerning cargo and inter-modal shipments;
- Identify and mitigate security risks within the supply chain through the Customs-Trade Partnership Against Terrorism (C-TPAT) program;
- Authorize the redirection of conveyances to other ports;
- Be aware of NOA changes provided by the Coast Guard;
- Ensure changes to the Trade Act of 2002 cargo manifest and Advance Passenger Information System (APIS) manifest for passenger and crewmembers are provided to the appropriate Coast Guard and CBP officials at alternate ports of entry;
- Consider temporary easement of enforcement of coastwise trade regulations to facilitate commerce;
- In coordination with DOS, approach the governments of Canada, Mexico, and Panama to make arrangements for diversion of U.S. bound cargo and passengers;
- Detect and identify chemical, biological, radiological, and nuclear materials through the employment of detection technology and coordination with CBP Weapons of Mass Destruction Teleforensics Center;
- Inspect cargo containers and review cargo information in advance of loading in foreign ports, through the Container Security Initiative (CSI);
- When requested, in accordance with agency authority and the availability of resources, redeploy appropriate personnel, equipment, air and marine assets and other resources in support;

- Participate in recovery activities of Area Maritime Security Committees;
- Support the Coast Guard so as to ensure compatibility, as appropriate, between the Customs-Trade Partnership Against Terrorism (C-TPAT) and requirements promulgated by the Coast Guard;
- Support the Coast Guard in planning Transportation Security Incident (TSI) recovery, as appropriate; and
- Provide support as outlined in ESFs 9, 10, 11, 13 of the NRP and any other tasking as directed by the Secretary of DHS.

Transportation Security Administration (TSA)

- Develop policies on the identification of critical assets and infrastructure;
- Coordinate with USCG, CBP, DOT, and private industry to facilitate redirection of conveyances to other ports;
- Following a TSI, in coordination with other appropriate stakeholders and government agencies, be aware of maximum available vessel, cargo and inter-modal capacity, to take steps to ensure the continuity of cargo flow;
- Monitor investigations of TSI's to obtain lessons learned to improve risk mitigation plans and programs.
- Support the Coast Guard in maritime security planning;
- Support the Coast Guard and participate as a member of the Area Maritime Security Advisory Committees;
- Coordinate intelligence functions with other entities of the DHS through the Transportation Security Operations Center (TSOC);
- Provide support as outlined in NRP and accompanying ESFs.

Emergency Preparedness and Response/Federal Emergency Management Agency (EP&R/FEMA)

- Provide disaster relief resources in accordance with the NRP.

Office of Intelligence and Analysis (I&A)

- Identify and assess a broad range of intelligence information concerning current and future threats against the United States;
- Issue timely warnings and advisories for the full spectrum of terrorist threats against the homeland, including physical and cyber events; and
- Review threats to the Maritime Transportation System (MTS) and marine critical infrastructure and key assets.

Directorate for Preparedness

- Consolidates preparedness assets across the Department:
- Facilitates grants and oversees nationwide preparedness efforts by supporting first responder training, citizen awareness, public health, infrastructure and cyber security and ensures proper steps are taken to protect high-risk targets:

- Focuses on cyber security and telecommunications:
- Addresses threats to our nation's public health through the Chief Medical Officer, who coordinates preparedness efforts against biological attacks: and
- Is responsible for infrastructure protection, training and exercises, the U.S. Fire Administration, and the Office of National Capitol Region Coordination.

Office of Operations Coordination

- Conducts joint operations across all organizational elements.
- Coordinates activities related to incident management.
- Employs all Department resources to translate intelligence and policy into action; and
- Oversees the Homeland Security Operations Center (HSOC) which collects and fuses information from more than 35 Federal, State, territorial, tribal, local, and private sector agencies.

Department of Defense (DoD)

- Provide Defense Support of Civil Authorities (DSCA) in accordance with the NRP;
- Support recovery activities with federal, state, local, and tribal elements as requested and approved by the Secretary of Defense;
- When requested and approved by the Secretary of Defense, provide military personnel, DoD civilians and contract personnel, as appropriate in support of domestic incidents; and
- Provide support under Immediate Response Authority by DoD directive and prior approval of the Secretary of Defense; and
- Take necessary "Immediate action" to respond to requests of civil authorities consistent with the Posse Comitatus Act.

U.S. Army Corps of Engineers (USACE)

- Provide rapid dredging capability through contracting or from Federal Dredging Fleet;
- Conduct high tech channel surveys;
- Conduct pre- and post-incident assessments of public works and infrastructure;
- Provide technical assistance to include engineering expertise, construction management and contracting, and real estate services;
- Provide emergency repair of damaged public critical infrastructure and facilities;
- Remove and dispose of contaminated and uncontaminated debris from public property;
- Provide appropriate representation to the IIMG and/or HSOC when requested by Office of Assistant Secretary of Defense for Homeland Defense;
- Restoration and operation of inland waterways, ports and harbors to include assisting in restoring the transportation infrastructure;
- Obtain heavy equipment and/or demolition services;
- Support mass care operations by providing ice, water and temporary housing;

- Temporary restoration of damaged public utilities by providing equipment, supplies and technical assistance;
- Recovery assistance to radiological and nuclear incidents to include radiological surveys, gross decontamination, site characterization, contaminated water management and site remediation;
- Assist with incident environmental impact assessments by providing technical environmental expertise;
- Deploy emergency power teams for power-system restoration;
- Provide long-term community recovery through community planning, civil engineering and hazard risk assessment expertise;
- Support development of national strategies and plans for the restoration of public facilities and infrastructure;
- Operational support for mobilization centers (including mobile command centers), staging areas, and distribution sites for all infrastructure and engineering service commodities; and
- Support the USCG and participate as an advisory member of the AMS Committees.

Department of State (DOS)

- Coordinate requests for, and offers of, transportation assistance from foreign governments;
- Provide support to the various ESFs, when activated, as outlined in the NRP;
- Notify foreign governments as appropriate of impacts on commerce ;
- In coordination with CBP, approach the governments of Canada, Mexico, and Panama to make arrangements for diversion and facilitation of U.S. bound cargo and passengers;
- Provide support of DHS Maritime and Cargo Security Programs; and
- Provide awareness and monitoring of cargo subject to export control.

Department of Transportation (DOT)

- Prioritize and/or allocate civil transportation capacity;
- Manage hazardous material containment response and movement;
- Assess damage to the nation's rail, pipeline and highway systems;
- Provide technical expertise and assistance for repair and restoration of transportation infrastructure;
- Provide advice and assistance on the transportation of contaminated materials;
- Provide engineering personnel and support to assist in damage and structural assessments, structural inspections and debris; and
- Provide support to the various ESFs, when activated, as outlined in the NRP.

Maritime Administration (MARAD)

- Provide transport of critical supplies, bulk goods, or heavy equipment/supplies to ports adjacent to disaster areas through the use of the National Defense Reserve Fleet;

- Obtain priority use and allocation of port facilities and services, shipping services, containers and chassis under the Defense Production Act;
- Maintain personnel readiness services needed to operate active and reserve vessels;
- Assist the USCG in development of recovery assessments and plans;
- Participate in activities of the Area Maritime Security Committees;
- Coordinate with CBP to determine if it is appropriate to waive provisions of the Jones Act; and
- Consider temporary easement of enforcement of coastwise trade regulations to facilitate commerce.

Federal Highway Administration (FHWA)

- Provide emergency funds or loans for repair or reconstruction of highways.

Federal Railroad Administration (FRA)

- Provide direct loans and guarantees to rehabilitate inter-modal or rail equipment or facilities.

St. Lawrence Seaway Development Corporation (SLSDC)

- Establish, operate, and maintain vessel traffic services; and
- Control or supervise vessel traffic.

Office of Pipeline Safety (OPS)

- Provide emergency funds or loans for repair or reconstruction of pipelines; and
- Coordinate recovery operations at the federal level for cross-modal aspects of a TSI;
- Respond to requests for waivers of restrictions to meet emergency requirements for pipeline operation.

Department of Interior (DOI)

- Provide tribal nation liaisons per ESF#3 of the NRP.

Department of Commerce (DOC)

- Provide economic impact data and analysis; and
- Provide to appropriate government agencies awareness and monitoring of cargo subject to export controls.

National Oceanic and Atmospheric Administration (NOAA)

- Assess port and regional level maritime, seafloor, weather and infrastructure conditions; and
- Provide awareness and monitoring information on maritime, seafloor weather and infrastructure conditions to appropriate incident management officials.

Department of Energy (DOE)

- Assist in the economic assessment of damage to energy infrastructure; and
- Consider use of Strategic Petroleum Reserve.

Department of Justice (DOJ)

- Through the FBI, conduct and coordinate all federal law enforcement and criminal investigation activities during a terrorist incident;
- Coordinate the activities of members of the law enforcement community; and
- Consult with other federal agencies with regard to the temporary easement of enforcement regulations to facilitate the reconstruction of critical infrastructure and resumption of commerce.

STATE, LOCAL AND TRIBAL GOVERNMENT

The MIRP recognizes that state, local and tribal governments using National Incident Management System principles have responsibility for incident management response and recovery efforts immediately after an incident. To manage their responsibilities, many of these government agencies currently have pre-established emergency response plans in place. However, recovery plans, especially for maritime infrastructure recovery and restoration of cargo flow, are not as prevalent. Many states engage individual task force groups to manage a myriad of disaster scenarios and response situations.

Due to the fact that the responsibilities, capabilities and organizational structures vary from agency to agency, it is difficult to establish specific functional responsibilities that each may be able to provide for recovery after a national TSI (or similarly disruptive incident). However, to coordinate the federal, state, local and tribal government relationship, the MIRP has identified a generic list of functional responsibilities for recovery that state, local, and tribal governmental agencies may perform.

State

- Coordinate state resources to address recovery;
- Make, amend, and rescind orders and regulations under certain emergency conditions in support of recovery efforts as appropriate;
- Communicate to the public recovery aspects of an emergency within state jurisdiction;
- Assist people, businesses, and organizations of the state cope with the consequences of recovery;
- Encourage participation in mutual aid and implement authorities for the state to enter into mutual aid agreements with other states, tribes, and territories to facilitate resource-sharing;
- Coordinate requests for federal assistance when it becomes clear that state or tribal capabilities will be insufficient or have been exceeded or exhausted;
- Engage in voluntary exchange of information with other federal, state, local and tribal government agencies;

- Participate in various advisory committees and task forces regarding recovery management;
- Assist in the assessment of the economic impact created by a security incident;
- Assist in the identification of recovery resources and assets; and
- Provide resources as requested and as appropriate.

Local

- Perform emergency first-responder activities as appropriate;
- Coordinate local resources to address recovery;
- Suspend local laws and ordinances, (dependent upon state and local law), under certain emergency conditions in support of recovery efforts as appropriate;
- Communicate to the public any type of declared emergency within local jurisdiction;
- Assist people, businesses, and organizations in the local area to cope with the consequences of any type of declared emergency and its recovery considerations;
- Negotiate and enter into mutual aid agreements with other jurisdictions to facilitate resource-sharing;
- Request state and, if necessary, federal assistance through the Governor of the State when the jurisdiction's capabilities have been exceeded or exhausted, or otherwise as appropriate;
- Engage in voluntary exchange of information with other federal, state local and tribal government agencies;
- Participate in various advisory committees and task forces regarding recovery management;
- Assist in the assessment of the economic impact created by a security incident;
- Assist in the identification of recovery resources and assets; and
- Provide resources as requested and as appropriate.

Tribal

- Coordinate local resources to address recovery;
- Suspend tribal laws and ordinances as appropriate;
- Communicate any type of declared emergency within tribal jurisdiction;
- Assist people, businesses, and organizations to cope with the consequences of any type of declared emergency;
- Negotiate and enter into mutual aid agreements with other tribes/jurisdictions to facilitate resource-sharing;
- Request state and federal assistance through the Governor of the State when the tribe's capabilities have been exceeded or exhausted;
- Deal directly with the federal government. (Although a state Governor must request a Presidential disaster declaration on behalf of a tribe under the Stafford Act, federal agencies can work directly with tribes within existing authorities and resources.)
- Engage in voluntary exchange of information with federal, state local and other tribal government agencies;
- Participate in various advisory committees and task forces regarding recovery management;

- Assist in the assessment of the economic impact created by a national TSI;
- Assist in the identification of recovery resources and assets; and
- Provide resources as requested and as appropriate.

PRIVATE SECTOR

The MIRP recognizes that the private sector/private industry plays a key role in the successful operation and management of the MTS. As the owner of the vast majority of the infrastructure assets, private sector entities have an important role in planning, operations, and advisory aspects relating to maritime infrastructure recovery and the restoration of passenger and cargo flow.

Following an incident that triggers implementation of this plan, the federal government will facilitate the restoration of commerce and recovery of the marine transportation infrastructure systems in concert with private sector contingency planning. To better prepare for this role, the MIRP advocates the following:

- Private sector owners and operators of vessels and facilities subject to U.S. government regulation are encouraged to expand their continuity of operations plans to include recovery operations as part of required planning pursuant to federal regulations, if such planning has not already been completed;
- Owners and operators of vessels and facilities not subject to U.S. government regulation are encouraged to establish recovery operations plans and submit them to their local Area Maritime Security Committee and the National Infrastructure Coordination Center's (NICC) Protected Critical Infrastructure Information (PCII) Program;
- All private sector recovery operations plans should include (1) a plan for evacuation, (2) adequate communications capabilities, and (3) a plan for continuity of operations;
- All private sector recovery operations plans should consider the existing American National Standard on Disaster/Emergency Management and Business Continuity Programs (NFPA 1600), which contains minimum criteria for disaster management and guidance in the development of a program for effective disaster preparedness response and recovery.

To assist in the development of recovery operations plans and other contingency planning, the following *Business Roundtable* guidance documents are recommended for private sector continuity of operations plan development:

- Committed to Protecting America: A Private-Sector Crisis Preparedness Guide, March 2005
- Committed to Protecting America: CEO Guide to Security Challenges, February 2005

It is anticipated that the private sector will implement continuity of operations plans/recovery operations plans on their own accord, based on incident information provided by the federal government. Information that may influence their decision to implement contingency plans and divert or redirect cargo and/or their conveyances are: national priorities; military requirements; MTS restrictions; and the expected duration of those restrictions.

To facilitate restoration of the flow of commerce and passenger vessel activity, the MIRP has identified a list of functional responsibilities that the private sector may perform:

- Engage in voluntary exchange of information about recovery operations plans with other potentially affected private sector entities and the federal government to mitigate potential congestion at non-incident site ports following the diversion of vessel traffic;
- Participate in various maritime industry stakeholder professional organizations and advisory committees such as the Area Maritime Security (AMS) Committees regarding recovery management and contingency planning (See Appendix A for AMS Planning Stakeholders);
- Assist in the assessment of economic impact;
- Assist in the identification of recovery resources and assets;
- Provide resources to assist in recovery, as appropriate;
- When requested by the National Maritime Security Advisory Committee (NMSAC), provide SMEs for advising on recovery management, especially regarding maritime salvage capability. (See Next Steps/Recommendations);
- Participate in pilot programs to test the effectiveness of the federal government to communicate recovery activities to the private sector (see Next Steps/Recommendations);
- Using existing information-sharing mechanisms such as the National Infrastructure Coordinating Center (NICC), Area Maritime Security (AMS) Committees, Transportation Sector Coordinating Council (SCC) and Information Sharing and Analysis Centers (ISAC), communicate situational and operational information as well as physical asset capabilities to the IIMG for mitigation management.

Government – Private Sector Information Sharing

In addition to performing various roles in recovery management, the private sector should be knowledgeable about information sharing and government-to-private sector coordinating mechanisms. Below is a list of several coordinating entities:

- DHS is enhancing sector-specific information sharing and coordinating mechanisms for all of the 17 critical infrastructure sectors, incorporating both Information Sharing and Analysis Centers (ISACs) and Sector Coordinating Councils (SCCs). These entities have dual roles in that they serve as central points of information sharing within each of the sectors and also act as the liaison to the federal government. One of the primary functions is to funnel threat information to facilities and receive and collect information from facilities.
- The Homeland Security Information Network - Critical Infrastructure (HSIN-CI) Pilot Program is an unclassified network that immediately provides the Department's Homeland Security Operations Center (HSOC) with one-stop, 24/7 access to a broad spectrum of industries, agencies and critical infrastructure across both the public and private sectors. This conduit for two-way information sharing provides the Department with an expanding base of locally knowledgeable experts and delivers real-time access to critical information. The HSIN-CI initiative was expanded to include critical infrastructure owners, operators and the private sector in all 50 states,

centered regionally around the cities of Dallas, Seattle, Indianapolis and Atlanta. To date, HSIN-CI communicates with nearly 40,000 members.

- National Infrastructure Coordinating Center (NICC): The mission of the NICC is to maintain operational awareness of the nation's critical infrastructure and key resources, and provide a mechanism and process for information sharing and coordination between and among government and industry partners. The NICC is the two-way communication flow point between DHS and private industry for reporting threats, events or crises that can potentially affect the successful operation of the nation's critical infrastructure and key resources. DHS use the NICC to provide private industry information about threats, warnings and defensive measures. Private industry uses the NICC to formally submit information that could affect or impede their continuous operations.
- Area Maritime Security (AMS) Committees: Established under the direction of the Captain of the Port (COTP) to provide advice and assist the development of the AMS Plan. Among other specified duties, the AMS Committee "shall serve as a link for communicating threats and changes in MARSEC Levels and disseminating appropriate security information to port stakeholders.

Using the flow chart below, the members of the private sector can see the organizations involved in the communications network for information flow between government and the private sector. (For further information, see Section IV – Concept of Operations and Next Steps/Recommendations about the communications network).

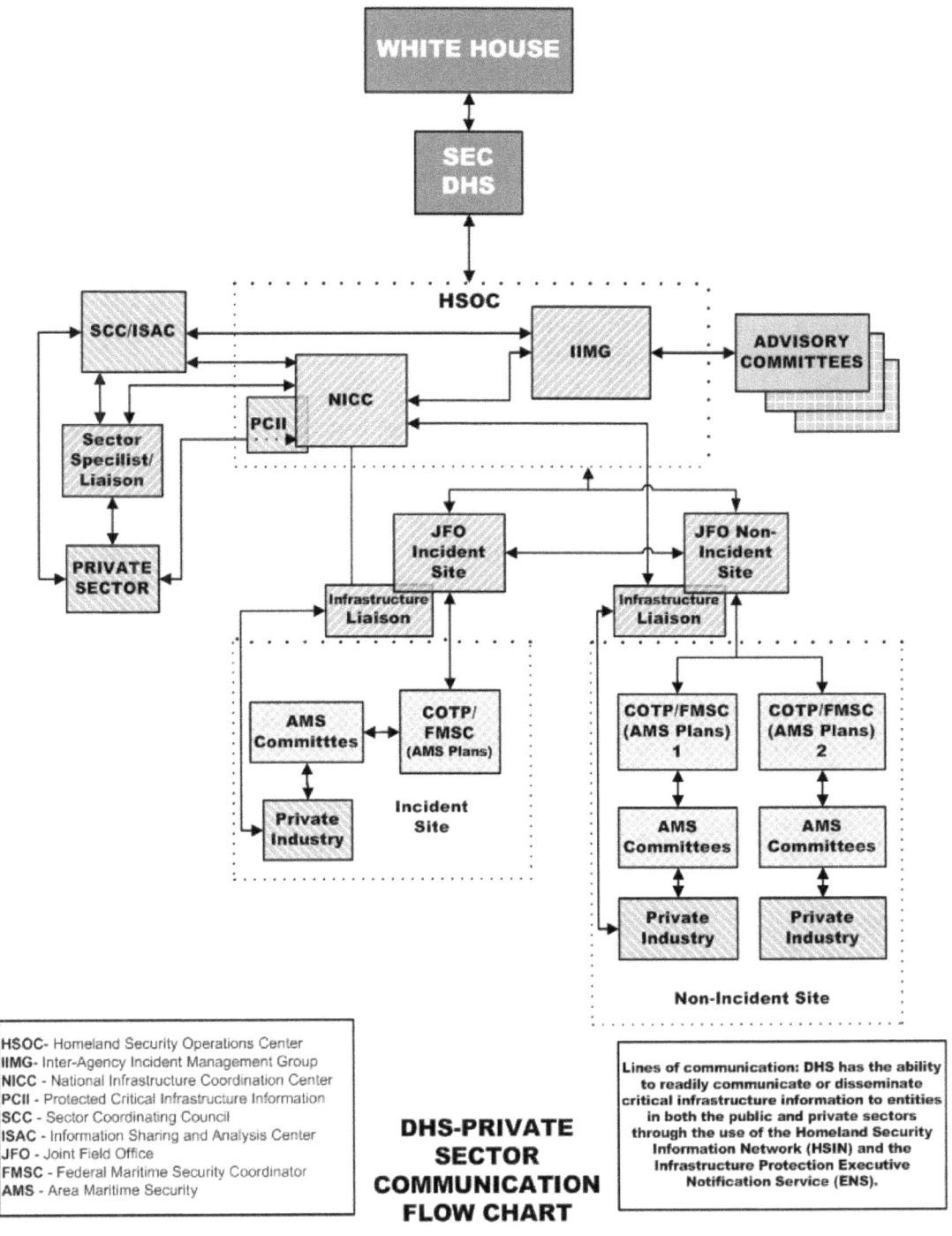

WHITE HOUSE

SEC DHS

HSOC

SCC/ISAC

IIMG

ADVISORY COMMITTEES

Sector Specilist/ Liaison

PCII

NICC

PRIVATE SECTOR

JFO Incident Site

JFO Non-Incident Site

Infrastructure Liaison

Infrastructure Liaison

AMS Committtes

COTP/ FMSC (AMS Plans)

COTP/FMSC (AMS Plans) 1

COTP/FMSC (AMS Plans) 2

Private Industry

Incident Site

AMS Committees

AMS Committees

Private Industry

Private Industry

Non-Incident Site

HSOC- Homeland Security Operations Center
IIMG- Inter-Agency Incident Management Group
NICC - National Infrastructure Coordination Center
PCII - Protected Critical Infrastructure Information
SCC - Sector Coordinating Council
ISAC - Information Sharing and Analysis Center
JFO - Joint Field Office
FMSC - Federal Maritime Security Coordinator
AMS - Area Maritime Security

DHS-PRIVATE SECTOR COMMUNICATION FLOW CHART

Lines of communication: DHS has the ability to readily communicate or disseminate critical infrastructure information to entities in both the public and private sectors through the use of the Homeland Security Information Network (HSIN) and the Infrastructure Protection Executive Notification Service (ENS).

Figure 3.1 – DHS-Private Sector Communication Flow Chart

IV. CONCEPT OF OPERATIONS

GENERAL

When an incident is of such severity, magnitude, and/or complexity that it is considered a national TSI and has been declared an Incident of National Significance (INS) according to the criteria established in the National Response Plan (NRP), the Secretary of Homeland Security (SecDHS), in coordination with other federal departments and agencies, initiates actions to prevent, prepare for, respond to, and recover from the incident. These actions are taken in conjunction with state, local, tribal, nongovernmental, and private-sector entities as appropriate to the threat or incident. (Any TSI that is declared an Incident of National Significance accordingly is referred to as a "national TSI.")

This section describes the federal coordinating structures, processes, and protocols employed to recover from a national TSI in the Maritime Transportation System (MTS). These coordinating structures and processes are aligned with the NRP, and enable execution of the responsibilities of the President through the appropriate federal departments and agencies, and to integrate federal, state, local, tribal, non-governmental organizations (NGO), and private-sector efforts into a comprehensive national approach to provide for public safety, the security of the MTS and to maintain and/or restore the flow of maritime commerce.

When faced with MTS restrictions, national-level decision-makers will facilitate scalable recovery activities concerning national maritime transportation infrastructure systems, specifically expediting the restoration of passenger and cargo flow to ports with capacity to accommodate cargo and inter-modal operations. The processes provided herein allow for MTS recovery activities to occur simultaneously with response activities at the incident site. If restricted from MTS participation during response operations, the incident site will be re-integrated into the MTS as part of its recovery operations.

OVERALL COORDINATION OF FEDERAL ACTIVITIES

During a national TSI, the overall coordination of federal incident management activities is executed through the Secretary of Homeland Security. Other federal departments and agencies carry out their incident management, emergency response, and recovery authorities, and responsibilities within this plan's overarching coordinating framework.

The Secretary of Homeland Security utilizes multi-agency structures at the headquarters, regional, and field levels to coordinate efforts, and provides appropriate support to the incident command structure.

At the federal headquarters level, incident information-sharing, operational planning, recovery, and deployment of federal resources are coordinated by the Homeland Security Operations Center (HSOC), and its component elements. Strategic-level interagency incident management coordination and Course of Action (COA) development are facilitated by the Interagency Incident Management Group (IIMG), which also serves as an advisory body to the Secretary of Homeland Security. Issues beyond the Secretary's authority to resolve are referred to the appropriate White House entity for resolution.

In the field, the Principal Federal Official (PFO) or the Federal Coordinating Officer (FCO), as appropriate, represents the Secretary of Homeland Security. Overall Federal support to the incident command structure on scene is coordinated through the Joint Field Office (JFO). For terrorist incidents, the Attorney General, acting through the FBI, executes the primary responsibilities for coordinating and conducting all federal law enforcement and criminal investigation activities. During a terrorist incident, the local FBI Special Agent-in-Charge (SAC), or FBI Headquarters designee, coordinates these activities with other members of the law enforcement community, and works in conjunction with the PFO, who coordinates overall federal incident management activities. The framework created by these coordinating structures is designed to accommodate the various roles of the federal government during and after an incident.

In the event of multiple incidents, a Unified Area Command may be established to oversee the management of multiple ICS organizations or to oversee the management of a very large or complex incident that has multiple incident management teams engaged. The simultaneous conduct of incident response and recovery operations, the restoration of passenger and cargo flow, add a new dimension for federal decision makers. Therefore, **a JFO, separate from the JFO supporting response operations at the incident site, may be established to support the coordination of recovery operations with federal, state, local, tribal, nongovernmental and private sector organizations.** This is consistent with the potential for the scope and complexity of an incident to create a demand for multiple JFO's. This need has been anticipated and is permitted by the NRP. (See page 28 of the NRP).

At the local level, on-scene incident command and management organization is located at the Incident Command Post (ICP). Designated incident management officials and responders from federal, state, local, and tribal agencies, as well as private-sector and nongovernmental organizations are typically onsite at the ICP. When multiple command authorities are involved in a response or recovery effort, the ICP may be led by a Unified Command, which is comprised of officials who have jurisdictional authority or functional responsibility for the incident under an appropriate law, ordinance, or agreement. The ICP will be located within the immediate vicinity of the incident site, the location having been selected by the primary jurisdictional authority. Each incident will generally have a unique ICP.

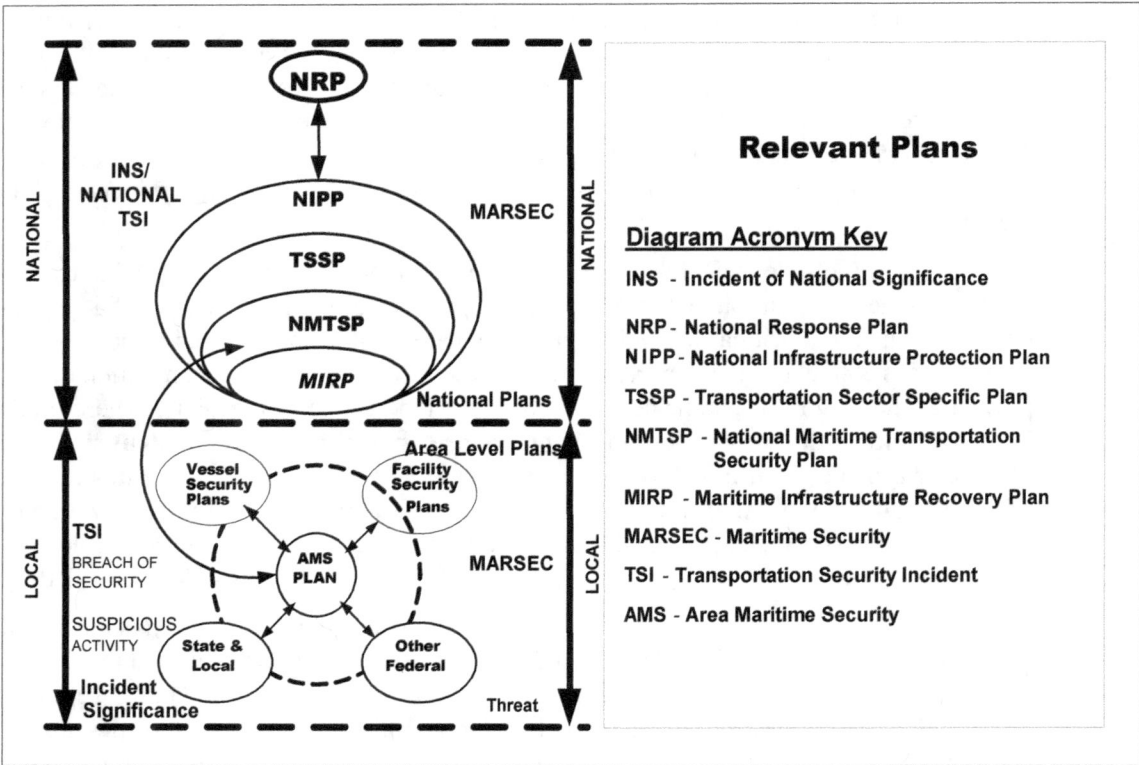

Figure 4.1 – MIRP Relationship to Relevant Plans

The MIRP is used as a post-incident recovery tool and details the federal coordinating guidelines during a national TSI. Many other plans work in concert with the MIRP to promote economic stability and protect continuity of commerce. Several examples of these plans follow:

- National Response Plan (NRP) – Recovery is the development, coordination, and execution of service and site restoration plans and the reconstitution of government operations and services through individual, private-sector, nongovernmental, and public assistance programs.
- National Infrastructure Protection Plan (NIPP) - A consistent, unifying structure for integrating critical infrastructure protection efforts into a national program. The NIPP outlines how DHS and its stakeholders will develop and implement the national effort to protect infrastructures across all sectors.
- Transportation Sector Specific Plan (TSSP) –To facilitate recovery and restoration activities following a TSI, the TSSP states the Sector Specific Responsibility (SSR) will work closely with DOT and other federal, state, and local agencies to remove regulatory impediments, reestablish supporting infrastructure, restore transportation service, and rebuild public confidence.

- National Maritime Security Plan (NMSP) – The NMSP functions as the capstone of the three-tiered system of domestic maritime security plans required under the Maritime Transportation Security Act (MTSA), comprised of: The National Maritime Security Plan; Area Maritime Security Plans prepared by Federal Maritime Security Coordinators; and Vessel and Facility Security Plans prepared by owners and operators. The NMSP serves also as the maritime sub-modal plan for the Transportation Sector Specific Plan (TSSP). The TSSP is one of 17 Sector and Key Asset plans required under the HSPD-7 National Infrastructure Protection Plan (NIPP).
- Area Maritime Security (AMS) Plans – The AMS Plans provide guidance for recovery of the Maritime Transportation System and reopening of the affected infrastructure, port(s) and/or waterways in the Area of Responsibility (AOR) following a transportation security incident. In the context of a national TSI, these AMS Plans may be implemented concurrently with other plans. In comporting with the NRP, the department or agency with primary responsibility for execution of AMS Plans is also responsible for ensuring that all ongoing activities conform to the processes and protocols prescribed in the NRP in responding to Transportation Security Incidents. This enables effective and coordinated federal incident management recovery with state, and local agencies, and relevant portions of the private sector authorities and responsibilities.

ORGANIZATIONAL ELEMENTS AND COORDINATION

The NRP, reflecting the National Incident Management System (NIMS), establishes a national structure for incident management: a clear progression of coordination and communication from the local level to regional to national headquarters level. The MIRP takes advantage of the organization in place under the NRP to conduct recovery operations. The following is a graphic representation of the information flow between local level activities and national recovery management:

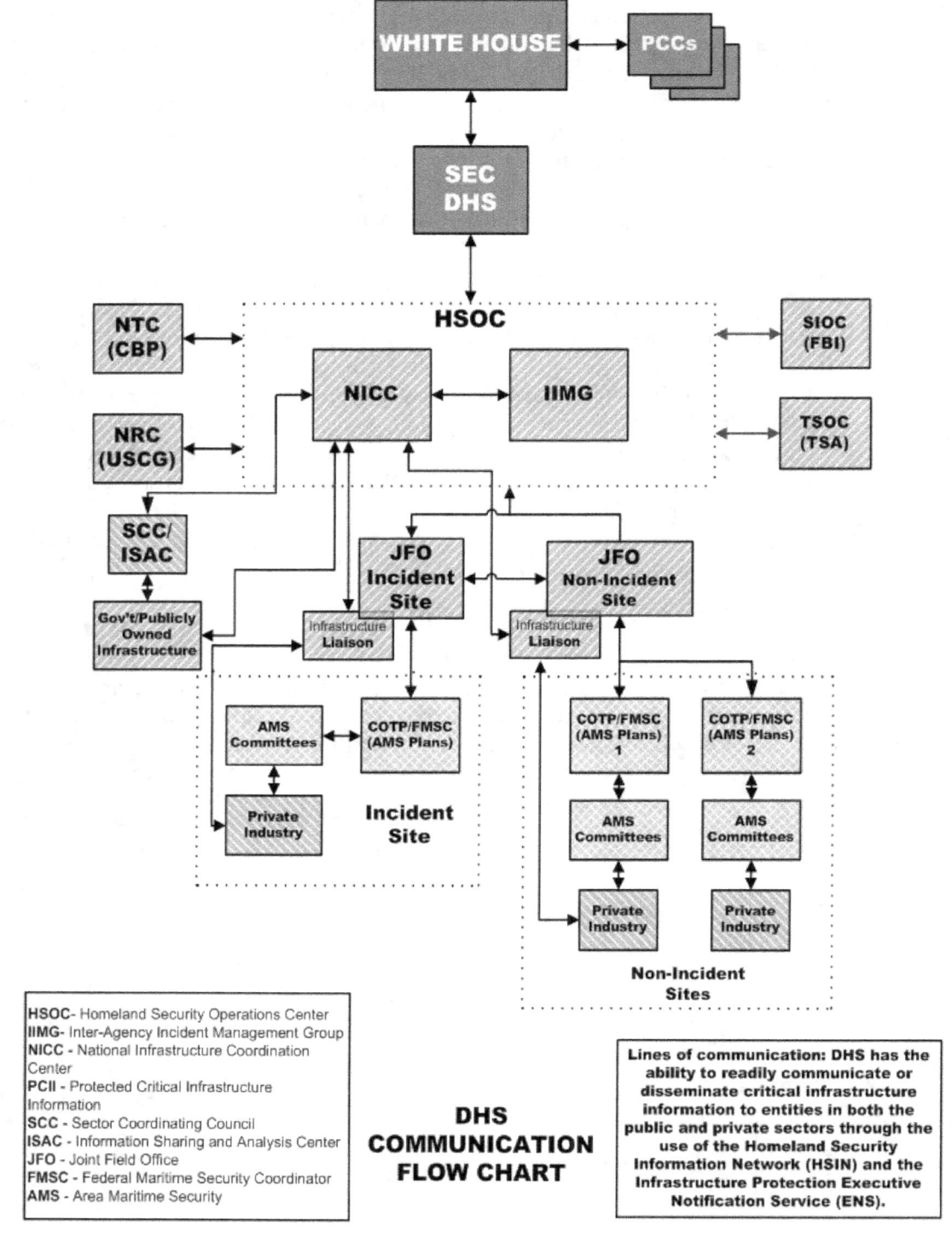

WHITE HOUSE ←→ PCCs

SEC DHS

HSOC

NTC (CBP)

NRC (USCG)

NICC ←→ IIMG

SIOC (FBI)

TSOC (TSA)

SCC/ISAC

Gov't/Publicly Owned Infrastructure

JFO Incident Site

Infrastructure Liaison

JFO Non-Incident Site

Infrastructure Liaison

AMS Committees

COTP/FMSC (AMS Plans)

Private Industry

Incident Site

COTP/FMSC (AMS Plans) 1

COTP/FMSC (AMS Plans) 2

AMS Committees

AMS Committees

Private Industry

Private Industry

Non-Incident Sites

HSOC- Homeland Security Operations Center
IIMG- Inter-Agency Incident Management Group
NICC - National Infrastructure Coordination Center
PCII - Protected Critical Infrastructure Information
SCC - Sector Coordinating Council
ISAC - Information Sharing and Analysis Center
JFO - Joint Field Office
FMSC - Federal Maritime Security Coordinator
AMS - Area Maritime Security

DHS COMMUNICATION FLOW CHART

Lines of communication: DHS has the ability to readily communicate or disseminate critical infrastructure information to entities in both the public and private sectors through the use of the Homeland Security Information Network (HSIN) and the Infrastructure Protection Executive Notification Service (ENS).

Figure 4.2 – DHS Communication Flow Chart

Principal Organizational Elements

This section describes the major organizational elements involved in federal recovery coordination. Further description of each of these elements can be found in Section IV of the National Response Plan.

Homeland Security Council/National Security Council

As stated in HSPD-5, the Assistant to the President for Homeland Security and the Assistant to the President for National Security Affairs are responsible for interagency policy coordination regarding domestic and international incident management, respectively, as directed by the President. Following an assessment by the Secretary of Homeland Security, those issues outside the authority of the Secretary, as defined in the Homeland Security Act, Stafford Act, and other relevant statutes, Executive orders, and directives, are elevated for resolution through the Homeland Security Council/National Security Council (HSC/NSC) system.

The Assistant to the President for Homeland Security and the Assistant to the President for National Security Affairs work together to ensure that domestic and international incident management efforts are seamlessly integrated.

Policy Coordination Committees (PCCs)

PCCs coordinate policy issues as part of the White House policy development process. NSPD-41/HSPD-13 established a Maritime Security PCC. PCCs may be convened at the request of any agency on an emergency basis based on a threat, a national TSI, or a policy issue of urgent nature.

Interagency Incident Management Group (IIMG)

The IIMG provides strategic situational awareness, synthesizes key intelligence and operational information, frames operational courses of action/policy, makes recommendations, anticipates evolving requirements, provides decision support to the Secretary of Homeland Security, and other national authorities (including the White House) during select periods of heightened alert and national-level domestic incidents.

Homeland Security Operations Center (HSOC)

The HSOC is the primary national hub for domestic incident-management coordination and situational awareness. The HSOC is a standing 24/7 interagency organization integrating law enforcement, national intelligence, emergency response, and private sector reporting. The HSOC facilitates homeland security information-sharing and operational coordination with other federal, state, local, tribal, and nongovernmental Emergency Operations Centers (EOCs).

The HSOC integrates elements of the DHS Office of the Assistant Secretary for Intelligence and Analysis (I&A) and DHS Emergency Preparedness and Response/Federal Emergency Management Agency (DHS/EPR/FEMA). These elements work in close coordination to address information/ intelligence analysis and response coordination.

HSOC (DHS Headquarters Facility Elements)

The HSOC convenes representatives from DHS and other federal departments and agencies to support steady-state threat-monitoring requirements and situational awareness and operational incident management coordination. The organizational structure of the HSOC is designed to integrate a full spectrum of interagency and private sector subject-matter expertise to meet the demands of a wide range of potential incident scenarios.

Intelligence/Information Analysis

In partnership with other elements of the HSOC, DHS/I&A/OIA is responsible for interagency intelligence collection requirements, analysis, production, and product dissemination for the DHS.

National Infrastructure Coordination Center (NICC)

The HSOC maintains communications and coordinates with critical infrastructure managers and key resources information-sharing entities through the National Infrastructure Coordination Center (NICC). The NICC monitors the Nation's critical infrastructure and key resources on an ongoing basis, and conducts daily polling of standing information-sharing entities for incidents and abnormalities. During an incident, the NICC is a coordinating vehicle for sharing information across infrastructure and key resource sectors through appropriate information-sharing channels. Associated with the NICC, the Protected Critical Infrastructure Information (PCII) Program is designed to encourage the private industry to share sensitive and proprietary business information with the government. PCII enables members of the private sector to voluntarily submit sensitive information regarding critical infrastructure with the assurance that the information will be protected from public disclosure.

Transportation Security Operations Center (TSOC)

TSA's TSOC monitors security-related developments around the clock. Information from intelligence organizations, open sources, and transportation industry sources is analyzed to provide real-time information to decision-makers, to determine changing threat conditions, and for decision-making for response and recovery. This information is coordinated with the HSOC, and shared with defense, law enforcement, and first-responder officials at all levels of government, as well as industry partners.

Strategic Information Operations Center (SIOC)

The FBI SIOC is the focal point and operational control center for all federal intelligence, law enforcement, and investigative law enforcement activities related to domestic terrorist incidents or credible threats, including leading attribution investigations. The SIOC serves as an information clearinghouse to help collect, process, vet, and disseminate information relevant to law enforcement and criminal investigation efforts in a timely manner. The SIOC maintains direct connectivity with the HSOC and IIMG. The SIOC, located at FBI Headquarters, supports the FBI's mission in leading efforts of the law enforcement community to detect, prevent, preempt, and disrupt terrorist attacks against the United States. The SIOC houses the National Joint Terrorism Task Force (NJTTF). The mission of the NJTTF is to enhance communications, coordination, and cooperation among federal, state, local, and tribal agencies representing intelligence, law enforcement, defense, diplomatic, public safety, and homeland security communities by providing a point of fusion for terrorism intelligence and by supporting Joint Terrorism Task Forces (JTTFs) throughout the United States. Recovery of damaged infrastructure cannot begin until investigative law activities have been completed by the SIOC.

National Response Center (NRC)

The NRC serves a very important role in the National Response System for the preservation, security and restoration of the environment and public safety as the conduit through which initial notification of response actions for various federal, state and local organizations takes place. The NRC's multi-disciplinary mission is to disseminate time critical information to first responders and government organizations about any reportable releases of oil and hazardous materials (HAZMAT) or potential releases (including chemical, biological, radiological agents and maritime terrorism related events) so as to ensure coordinated and appropriate incident response.

National Targeting Center (NTC)

The NTC is the centralized coordination point to provide tactical targeting and analytical research in support of CBP anti-terrorism efforts.

DOT Crisis Management Center (CMC)

The DOT CMC continually monitors the national transportation system across all modes for threats, incidents, or events involving safety, mobility and security. This includes accidents, hazardous materials incidents and transportation impacts resulting from weather, natural disasters or security threats or events. The CMC monitors international events where DOT either has a presence or there is a potential nexus for the domestic transportation system. This information is provided to and coordinated with the HSOC, and security-related reports are shared with TSA through the TSOC or the TSA representative to the HSOC.

Department of Defense (DoD) Coordination

The Department of Defense has significant resources that may be available to support any federal response to a national TSI. The Secretary of Defense authorizes Defense Support of Civilian Authorities (DSCA) for domestic incidents as directed by the President or when consistent with military readiness operations and appropriate under the circumstances and the law. The Secretary of Defense retains command of military forces under DSCA, as with all other situations and operations. DoD provides DSCA in accordance with the National Response Plan (NRP).

International Coordination

The Department of State (DOS) conducts international coordination between the U.S. government, foreign nations, and international and regional organizations in support of the MIRP.

Regional Organizational Elements and Coordination

Some national TSIs may be managed primarily using regional resources, with national-level monitoring. In large-magnitude, high-visibility, and/or sensitive situations, the Joint Field Office (JFO) is activated to coordinate directly with the national-level HSOC and IIMG. The JFO is a multi-agency coordination center established locally. It provides a central location for coordination of federal, state, local, tribal, non-governmental, and private sector organizations with primary responsibility for threat response and incident recovery support. The JFO enables the effective and efficient coordination of federal incident-related prevention, preparedness, response, and recovery actions.

Headquarters/national-level elements must closely monitor regional recovery operations planning and remain prepared to assist if the required resources exceed those available through the JFO.

Joint Field Office (JFO) Organization Components

JFO Coordination Group

Utilizing the NIMS principle of Unified Command, JFO activities are directed by a JFO Coordination Group, which may include the Principal Federal Officer, Federal Coordinating Officer, Senior Federal Law Enforcement Official, and/or other Senior Federal Officials with primary jurisdictional responsibility or functional authority for incident management. The JFO Coordination Group also includes a limited number of principal state, local, and tribal officials (such as the State Coordinating Officer (SCO)), as well as non-governmental organizations (NGO) and private-sector representatives. The JFO Coordination Group functions as a multi-agency coordination entity and works jointly to establish priorities, allocate resources, resolve interagency policy issues, and provide strategic guidance to support federal incident management activities. The JFO Coordination Group develops strategic guidance and facilitates resolution of conflicts in priorities for allocation of critical federal resources. If policy issue resolution cannot be achieved between JFO Coordination Group members, issues may be raised to the IIMG or through appropriate agency chains of command for consideration by higher authorities. It should be noted that a JFO, separate from the JFO supporting response operations for an incident site, may be established to coordinate recovery operations with federal, state, local, tribal, nongovernmental and private sector organizations.

Principal Federal Officer (PFO)

The PFO is personally designated by the Secretary of Homeland Security to facilitate federal support to the established Incident Command System (ICS)/Unified Command structure (UCS) and to coordinate overall federal incident management and assistance activities across the spectrum of prevention, preparedness, response, and recovery.

Federal Coordinating Officer (FCO)

The FCO manages and coordinates federal resource support activities related to Stafford Act disasters and emergencies. In Stafford Act situations where a PFO has not been assigned, the FCO provides overall coordination for the Federal components of the JFO and works in partnership with the State Coordinating Officer (SCO) to determine and satisfy state, and local assistance requirements.

Senior Federal Law Enforcement Official (SFLEO)

The SFLEO is the senior law enforcement official from the agency with primary jurisdictional responsibility, as directed by statute, Presidential directive, existing federal policies, and/or the Attorney General. The SFLEO directs intelligence/investigative law enforcement operations related to the incident and supports law enforcement components of the Unified Command on-scene. In the event of a terrorist incident, this official will normally be the FBI Special Agent-in-Charge.

State/Local/Tribal Official(s)

The JFO Coordination Group also includes state representatives, such as the SCO, who serves as the state counterpart to the FCO in managing the state's incident management programs and activities, and the Governor's Authorized Representative (GAR), who represents the Governor of the affected state. The JFO Coordination Group may also include tribal and/or local area representatives with primary statutory authority for incident management.

Senior Federal Officials (SFO)

The JFO Coordination Group may also include officials representing other federal departments or agencies with primary statutory responsibility for certain aspects of incident management. SFOs utilize existing authorities, expertise, and capabilities to assist in management of the incident working in coordination with the PFO, FCO, SFLEO, and other members of the JFO Coordination Group. When appropriate, the JFO Coordination Group may also include U.S. attorneys or other senior officials, or their designees, from the DOJ to provide expert legal counsel.

Infrastructure Liaison

Designated by the DHS Directorate for Preparedness Office of Infrastructure Protection (IP), and assigned to the JFO Coordination Staff, the Infrastructure Liaison serves as the principal advisor to the JFO regarding all Critical Infrastructure/Key Asset (CI/KA) incident related issues, communicating with the IP representative at the IIMG, NRCC and NICC, and coordinating with the private sector.

Area Organization Components

Federal Maritime Security Coordinators (FMSCs)

FMSCs are the U.S. Coast Guard Captains of the Port (COTP) who serve as local officers exercising authority for COTP zones described in 33 CFR Part 3. The COTP is the FMSC described in 46 U.S.C 70103(a) (2) (G). COTP/FMSCs are charged with the responsibility of establishing AMS Committees and developing Area Maritime Security (AMS) Plans. This security responsibility is in addition to key responsibilities for traditional Coast Guard missions and is fundamental to the success of the Maritime Homeland Security program. COTP/FMSCs rely on federal, state, and local agencies, and other maritime area partners to assist in planning and implementation of security plans. COTP/FMSCs are authorized to establish, convene, and direct the AMS Committees, appoint members to AMS Committees;

develop and maintain, in coordination with AMS Committees, the AMS Plans; and implement and exercise AMS Plans.

Area Maritime Security (AMS) Committees

AMS Committees, established under 33 CFR Part 103, assist in the development, review, and updating of AMS Plans. The AMS Committees bring together appropriate experienced government/industry representatives from a variety of sources in their region to continually assess security risks to the ports, determine appropriate risk mitigation strategies, and develop, revise, and implement AMS plans. AMS Committees also serve as mechanisms by which security threats and changes in MARSEC and DHS Threat Levels are communicated to maritime stakeholders.

NATIONAL – REGIONAL COORDINATION AND PROCEDURES

A basic concept of NIMS, and therefore the MIRP, is that incidents are generally handled at the lowest jurisdictional level possible. In instances regarding maritime transportation infrastructure, a federal agency may act as a first-responder and may provide direction or assistance specific to its statutory authorities and responsibilities. In the vast majority of maritime incidents, Area Maritime Security (AMS) Plans provide incident prevention, response, and recovery guidance. During a national TSI, the Secretary of Homeland Security, in coordination with other federal departments and agencies, initiates actions to deal with incident management at the national level. At the national level, the Coast Guard Commandant and the Customs and Border Protection Commissioner will determine appropriate initial measures for response (prevention and protection) and recovery activities at ports, other than the incident site(s), throughout the country.

Recovery operations will normally follow initial tactical and short-term, targeted operational actions taken by senior Coast Guard and Customs and Border Protection leadership to direct a security posture immediately following a maritime TSI in one or more ports, waterways, or coastal approaches. A prudent and measured response will be taken based on an assessment, including available intelligence, of the specific incident. The MTS should not be shut down as an automatic response to a maritime incident. Their decisions may transcend Coast Guard AORs, significantly impact maritime industry, change the Maritime Security (MARSEC) Level, and perhaps affect/involve other DHS agencies and departments, prevent further attacks, protect CI/KA, and maintain the flow of commerce through non-incident sites.

This section complements the concepts of the National Maritime Security Plan (NMSP) by providing procedures for managing recovery operations on a long-term basis. The procedures are general in nature; specific guidance is impractical. With over 2,100 possible threat scenarios in hundreds of ports, the variables affecting maritime infrastructure recovery are too myriad to provide detailed procedures.

National and Regional level Recovery Management Procedures

The general procedures herein assist the Joint Field Office (JFO) and the Interagency Incident Management Group (IIMG), or other delegated representatives of the Secretary of Homeland Security, in addressing the most important recovery factors to maintain the flow of maritime commerce and mitigate the effects of terrorist incidents on the economy of the United States.

<u>First Step: Receive up-to-date Current Common Operating Picture (COP).</u>

Once formed, the JFO and/or IIMG must make a quick assessment of the economic sensitivities and ramifications of the incident. Early recovery of maritime commerce will be essential to protect the economic health of the nation. Recovery operations must be addressed by the IIMG if the impact at the incident site requires resources beyond the scope of the responding JFO and COTP/FMSCs. The following topics represent information needed by the JFO or the IIMG to assist in early assessment of recovery needs:

- Incident information
    - Type event
    - Location (where, when)
    - Size: extent of damage
- Initial government targeted response actions
    - Initial and current Control Actions
    - Current MARSEC Level
    - DHS Homeland Security Alert System (HSAS) Threat Condition Alert Level
    - Current Deny-Entry status (have any maritime conveyances/cargo been diverted?)
- Incident site:
    - Current Status
    - Affected Infrastructure (include inter-modal connections)
    - Expected duration of conveyance restriction(s) (if applicable)

<u>Second Step: Review personnel and adjust JFO/IIMG membership as appropriate.</u>

- JFO Operations Section reviews the makeup of the Recovery Branch Personnel.
- In accordance with the NRP, a core group of agencies and departments are represented when the IIMG is convened. The IIMG is a scalable organization and would be augmented with SMEs to assist with the recovery of a national TSI. The SME component should be sufficient to assist the IIMG to define the incident impact, identify required recovery resources and to identify private industry members to participate in restoration of passenger and cargo flow operations. All of the federal departments along with many of the agencies listed in Section III of this plan are represented in the IIMG Core Group.

<u>Third Step: Assess impact on the National Maritime Transportation System (MTS).</u>

Use Subject Matter Experts (SMEs) from various sources -- government, maritime industry (trade) associations or advisory committees -- to assess the extent of damage to the MTS and estimate the duration of the impact (i.e., short term to long term) on recovery activities. The duration of the restriction is the key element to assessing the scale of the impact to the MTS and in deciding to initiate recovery of commerce operations at alternate sites while the national TSI site is still in the response phase. The following topics should be considered to assess the impact on the MTS:

- What types of conveyances/cargoes have been restricted?
  - Container Vessels
  - Dry Bulk Vessels
  - Liquid Bulk Vessels
  - Break Bulk Vessels
  - Barges
  - Lash Barges
  - Passenger Vessels
  - Roll On / Roll Off Vessels
  - Other vessels
- What is the extent of conveyance/cargo restriction at the national TSI site?
  - Full
  - Partial (may be expressed in %)
- What is the relevance of the national TSI site to the MTS?
  - Port
    - Large % of regional or national cargo throughput.
      (The combined ports of Los Angeles and Long Beach, CA, handle 32% of the nation's container throughput.)
    - Large % of regional or national reserve cargo-handling capacity.
      (The port of New Orleans, while totaling 1% of the nation's container throughput, accounts for 14% of the nation's container reserve capacity.)
    - Sole source of supply to geographic isolated area.
      (Hawaii and Puerto Rico are dependent upon the ports of Honolulu and San Juan, respectively, though they account for a small percentage of national trade.)
    - Large % of key commodity throughput.
      (The United States holds less than 4% of the world's Liquid Natural Gas (LNG) resources. The United States operates only four LNG terminals; the largest is in Cove Point, MD.)
    - Port is militarily strategic.
  - Is there a Critical Infrastructure/Key Asset (CI/KA) (other than port) involved?
    - Key waterway.
      (The Houston Ship Channel provides sole maritime access to the Port of Houston.)
    - Key facility (sole/major commodity source).
      (The Louisiana Offshore Crude Oil Port (LOOP) takes in 13% of U.S. crude oil imports.)
- What is the duration of the conveyance/cargo restriction(s)?
  - Duration is not a finite factor; the acceptable duration of conveyance/cargo restriction will vary with each national TSI. Diversion of conveyance/cargo for energy supply or perishable foods will have relatively shorter acceptable restriction durations than a barge moving dry bulk goods on the inland

waterways. Each national TSI impact must be assessed individually to determine what constitutes an acceptable duration of conveyance/cargo restriction prior to diverting conveyances within the MTS.

<u>Fourth Step: Determine scale of the national TSI impact on the National Maritime Transportation System (MTS).</u>

- The scale of the national TSI impact is defined as escalating degrees of severity, each requiring increasing resources to conduct recovery operations. A hierarchy of increasing impact scale is provided below:
    - <u>Local</u>: The national TSI impact is contained within an AOR. The COTP/FMSC has sufficient resources to manage recovery operations within sufficient time to avoid the diversion of conveyances/cargo to an alternate port. In the case of local recovery, the JFO will monitor recovery efforts, be prepared to assist with out-of-area resources if requested by the COTP/FMSC and monitor the MTS and private sector infrastructure through the National Infrastructure Coordinating Center (NICC).
    - <u>Regional</u>: Recovery from a national TSI impact can be addressed within the resources of the five major maritime regions: West Coast, East Coast, Gulf Coast, Great Lakes and Inland Rivers. In the case of local or regional recovery, the IIMG will monitor recovery efforts, be prepared to assist with out-of-area resources if requested by the JFO and monitor the MTS and private sector infrastructure through the National Infrastructure Coordinating Center (NICC).
    - <u>National</u>: Recovery from national TSI impact can be addressed domestically from two or more of the five major maritime regions.
    - <u>International</u>: Recovery requirements of the national TSI impact exceed domestic resources. Some examples of International assistance are:
        - Use of Canadian (Vancouver and/or Halifax) port reserve capacity/cargo-handling capacity and inter-modal connections to reestablish the flow of maritime commerce.
        - Use of Mexican ports for temporary storage of goods or transfer of cargo to vessels capable of passage through the Panama Canal. Mexican port inter-modal connections are inadequate for use in lieu of US port(s)[2].
        - A substantial restriction and loss of MTS capacity may require DOS to inform conveyance originating nation(s) of impending MTS restrictions.
- Facilitate government assistance if the impact to the MTS at the incident site exceeds the resources of the FMSC/AMS Committees, state, local, and other local federal response resources. (See Section III – Roles and Responsibilities for functional responsibilities of various organizations involved in recovery. Refer to the NRP for capabilities of federal agencies under NRP ESFs). *If the impact is contained within*

---

[2]Coast Guard Intelligence Report CG-FPT-054-03, West Coast Containerized Cargo Alternate Ports Analysis dated July 2003, page 9.

the geographic boundaries of a COTP zone, the cognizant COTP/FMSC will implement recovery operations using the Area Maritime Security (AMS) Plan.

- The JFO will perform incident support functions if the scale of recovery exceeds the resources of the cognizant COTP(s). If recovery operations exceed the JFO resources, the PFO requests assistance through the HSOC. Consult the Department of State (DOS) anytime the impact requires recovery resources that exceed national capabilities. Include the DOS in recovery planning as soon as the need arises or is anticipated.

Fifth Step: Determine incident-based National/Regional priorities, as appropriate.

- Decision makers must recognize that import/export priorities may need to be set to facilitate recovery and other government, public and private activities. Maritime commerce should be prioritized and communicated to meet identified needs, to facilitate incident management activities and support military operations. COTPs should be given authority for minor deviations from these priorities in order to maximize port efficiencies, providing for the best match of conveyance, cargo and port resources. Priorities may cover, but are not exclusive to:
  o Emergency Needs: those goods necessary for the saving and continuation of life. Examples include personnel and supplies for: medical response, restoration of power and potable water.
  o Response Needs: Personnel and equipment necessary to conduct response operations at the incident site (i.e. fire boats).
  o Commodity Needs: The incident may create immediate shortages of necessary commodities that must be addressed. Examples are: crude oil, heating oil and chemicals necessary for production and drinking water. Commodity needs may also have a delayed time component based upon "on-hand" stocks. COTPs and national Advisory Committees must be queried to identify these commodities.
  o Military Requirements.

Sixth Step: Determine Maritime Trade restrictions resulting from the national TSI.

These limitations are a combination of conveyance restrictions, government actions and priorities. These restrictions will need to be communicated to the private sector for appropriate and timely execution of their continuity of operations/contingency plans.

MTS information provided to the private sector is presented as restrictions to trade to make the information easily manageable and understandable. Also, the authorities of DHS agencies to control all access to territorial waters of the United States are normally exclusionary in nature. Sources of maritime trade restrictions are:

- Damage to MTS Infrastructure
- Port State Control
- Military Out Load

- MARSEC level (security requirements)
- DHS HSAS threat levels
- National/Regional priorities
- Defense Production Act (DPA) priorities
- Restrictions/priorities resulting from implementation of National Emergencies Act

<u>Seventh Step: Communicate with the Private Sector.</u>

Due to the nature of the MTS, with a variety of commerce and conveyances operating through hundreds of ports located on inland waterways and coasts, this plan recognizes that private sector interests will be specific to each incident. The IIMG and/or JFO should use participating SMEs (see Second Step) to identify those affected in the maritime community by the national TSI. Additional key industry members may be identified by AMS Committees in the affected region(s) and invited to participate as SMEs. The identified private sector/industry members should have the authority to share information and resolve conflicting business continuity plans with other industry members. The IIMG and/or the JFO should provide the private sector with information on the national TSI situation, impact, and MTS restrictions with emphasis on impact to maritime commerce. To gather information at the incident site, the responsible COTP/FMSCs may be queried through the HSOC. The following are key issues regarding communication:

- Communicate information, as necessary, regarding what MTS infrastructure is available to accommodate movement of vessels and loading and offloading of cargo and/or passengers.
- To avoid exceeding throughput capacity at a recovery location, encourage voluntary exchange of information about specific recovery operations/continuity plans among private sector companies, and facilitate close coordination with federal decision makers.

This plan recognizes that a need may exist to engage the private sector for two-way information sharing. The following organizations provide conduits for information from government to the private sector (and vice versa):

- Transportation Sector Coordinating Council (SCC): The February 2005 Interim NIPP established private sector SCCs for the Nation's CI/KA sectors. The purpose of the SCCs is to provide the framework for private-sector owners and operators to engage DHS and the Sector Specific Agencies (SSAs) and to collaborate with them to (1) identify, prioritize, and coordinate the protection of CI/KA, and (2) facilitate sharing of information about threats, vulnerabilities, incidents, potential protective measures, and best practices.

- Area Maritime Security (AMS) Committee: Established under the direction of the Captain of the Port (COTP) to provide advice and assist the development of the AMS Plan. Among other specified duties, the AMS Committee "shall serve as a link for communicating threats and changes in MARSEC Levels and disseminating appropriate security information to port stakeholders." [3]

---

[3] 33 CFR Navigation and Navigable Waters, Chapter I, Subchapter H, Part 103, Section 103.310(b)

<u>Eighth Step:</u> The IIMG and /or JFO develop Recovery strategies and COAs for submission to the Secretary of Homeland Security or Principal Federal Official, as appropriate. Include:

- Scale of recovery resources.
- Recommended changes for the Homeland Security Advisory System (HSAS) Threat Condition (IIMG recommendation only).
- Recommended Maritime Security (MARSEC) Level. Commandant, U.S. Coast Guard sets the MARSEC Level consistent with the equivalent Homeland Security Advisory System (HSAS) Threat Condition and that Threat Condition's scope of application. Notwithstanding the HSAS, the Commandant retains the discretion to adjust the MARSEC Level when necessary to address any particular security concerns or circumstances related to maritime elements of the national transportation system.[4]

Recommended changes to the MARSEC level, and therefore security posture, should be informed by threat-based, consequence-driven risk analysis as described in Appendix B. Risk management must be applied to ensure public safety and supply chain security before maritime cargo flow can be resumed. Risk will never be eliminated but can be managed to an acceptable level, which must be established for each incident. The MARSEC Level will define the vulnerability of the MTS and must be at a level to maintain the minimal acceptable risk. Decision makers must remain cognizant that private industry security measures are linked to the MARSEC Level. Potential strategic and COAs are listed below:

- Temporary easements of enforcement of appropriate regulatory requirements.
- Recommended use of CBP programs to assist screening efforts. CBP has developed and deployed a number of initiatives to detect and prevent terrorists and terrorist weapons from entering the United States. The initiatives can assist the maritime recovery screening process to maximize limited resources without increasing risk.
    - o Personnel:
        - Advance Passenger Information System (APIS): APIS is an automated system capable of performing database queries on passengers and crewmembers prior to their arrival in or departure from the United States.
        - Electronic Notice of Arrival/Departure System (NOAD): Joint USCG – CBP program provides the maritime industry with one avenue to submit required vessel, crew, and passenger information.
    - o Container Cargo
        - 24-Hour Rule/Trade Act of 2002: Cargo information must be received by CBP 24 hours prior to lading at a foreign port.
        - Container Security Initiative: Bilateral, reciprocal agreements that position CBP personnel at selected foreign ports to pre-screen United States bound containers.
        - Customs-Trade Partnership Against Terrorism (C-TPAT): A partnership between CBP and industry built on trust and a demonstrated commitment to supply chain security. Program acceptance is based upon a broad range

---

[4] 33 CFR Navigation and Navigable Waters, Chapter I, Subchapter H, Part 101, Section 101.405

of security topics including personnel; physical and procedural security; access controls; education, training and awareness; manifest procedures; conveyance security; threat awareness; and documentation processing.

- Automated Targeting System (ATS): The premier enforcement targeting tool utilized by CBP to screen inbound cargo shipments to the United States. ATS is an evolving, flexible system; targeting rules can be adjusted to include the latest intelligence such as post-incident forensics.

<u>Ninth Step: Implement chosen Strategy/COA.</u>

<u>Tenth Step: Measure outcomes and effectiveness of implemented Strategy/COA; adjust actions as necessary.</u>

<u>Eleventh Step: Monitor local recovery efforts at the national TSI site and facilitate reintegration of the incident site into the MTS as applicable.</u>

<u>Twelfth Step: Facilitate restoration of the MTS functional capacity to pre-national TSI levels.</u>

RECOVERY MANAGEMENT SUPPORT BY NON-INCIDENT SITES

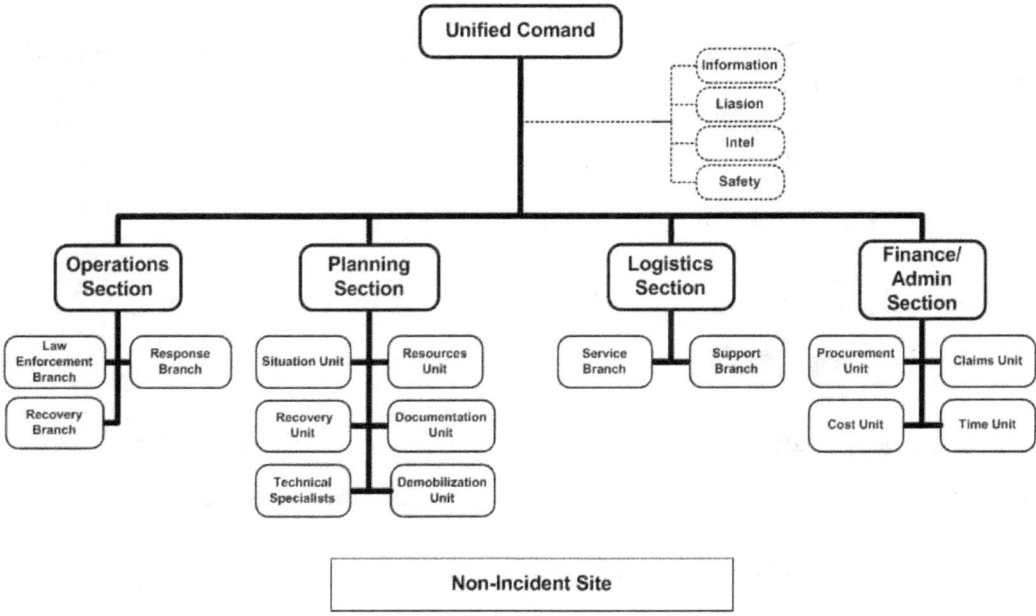

Figure 4.3 - Maritime Infrastructure Recovery Sample Organization Chart for **Non**-Incident Site

This section describes considerations for recovery at sites other than the incident site. These considerations are intended for use by COTP/ FMSCs at non-incident sites. Proactive development of information and capabilities at these sites may significantly reduce commerce recovery time and minimize damage to the economy of the United States. It is important that actions taken by the COTP/FMSCs at non-incident sites be communicated to decisions makers at the regional and national levels to ensure that COAs are coordinated. The following should be included in non-incident site recovery considerations:

- COTP/FMSCs should anticipate and prepare for requests for information, assistance and/or resources from the JFO or the IIMG. When the MTS has been damaged to the extent that cargo flow needs to be redirected, COTP/FMSCs should work with all levels of government as well as the private sector to identify and increase port and waterway maximum capacities. In the extreme case where the flow of passengers and cargo has been interrupted, COTPs must develop AOR specific impact information. Federal decision makers must be informed of the risk resulting from the interruption of commerce to accurately balance security measures and damage to the economy.

- Immediately following a national TSI, ports at sites other than the incident site may be significantly affected due to the re-direction of maritime traffic and cargos. COTP's may need to be responsive to regional and/or national needs that the IIMG or the PFO may establish through prioritization criteria for ports other than the incident site.
  o To manage incident-specific risk, "the COTP may temporarily raise the MARSEC Level for the port, a specific marine operation within the port,

or a specific industry within the port, when necessary to address an exigent circumstance immediately affecting the security of the maritime elements of the transportation system in his/her area of responsibility."[3]

- o The COTP/FMSC should consider establishing a Unified Command (see sample above) using the principles contained in the National Incident Management System (NIMS). The Unified Command (UC) will provide needed SMEs and mobilize appropriate federal, state, local and tribal governments and private sector organizations to support larger scale MTS recovery operations. Representatives from other transportation sectors, such as highway and rail, and the private sector should be included in the UC as appropriate. *Potential UC members should be identified in advance and be provided training in the principles of NIMS.*
- COTP/FMSCs, in close cooperation with port authorities and maritime industry stakeholders, should determine the maximum conveyance, cargo and passenger capacities for their areas of responsibilities. Determining maximum capacities (and capabilities) is not a simple task. It will require participation from all levels of the MTS and will include inter-modal connections and capacities.
  - o Several variables of maximum capacity to consider are general to maritime commerce:
    - Port Centric
      - Anchorage capacity.
      - Barge fleet facilities.
      - Approach channels and berthing access: width and depth.
      - Vessel-to-Apron Capacity: technology, equipment and compatibility.
      - Apron to Storage: equipment, distances and capacities.
      - Storage to Rail or Gate: distances, rail yard and gate capacities, number of drivers.
      - Labor constraints: physical and contractual.
    - Waterways
      - Function: Who normally uses the waterway?
      - Depth and width.
      - Chokepoints: natural and manmade.
      - Inter-modal connections.
      - Barge fleet facilities.
      - Number of barges and operators.
  - o Certain forms of maritime commerce will have variables of maximum capacity that are specific to that commerce:
    - Passenger
      - Facility for disembarkation.
      - Passenger holding area.
      - Transportation to inter-modal transportation connections.
      - Capacities of rail, bus and airlines.

---

[3] 33 CFR Navigation and Navigable Waters, Chapter I, Subchapter H, Part 101, Section 101.200(d).

- CBP inspection resources.
  - Liquid bulk: crude oil.
    - Storage capacity.
    - Pipeline capacity.
    - Refinery capacity.
  - Containers.
    - Storage: stacking.
    - Exports: full and empty containers.
    - Labor: labor intensive, maximum capacity must avoid surge burnout.
    - CBP inspection resources.
- Intermodal considerations: once the maritime maximum capacities have been identified, COTPs must ensure that the intermodal connections and systems are capable of equivalent capacities.

RECOVERY MANAGEMENT AT THE NATIONAL TSI SITE

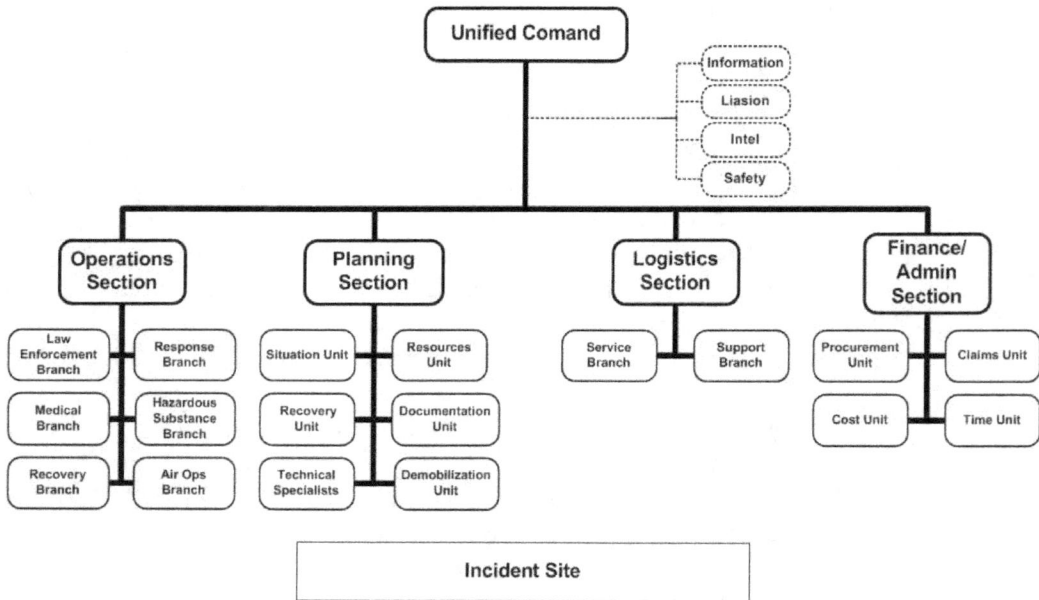

Figure 4.4 - Maritime Infrastructure Recovery Sample Organization Chart for Incident Site

Introduction

This section describes planning considerations and general recovery procedures to complement incident management procedures addressed in Area Maritime Security (AMS) Plans and used at the incident site. AMS Plans are developed and used by Federal Maritime Security Coordinators (FMSCs) in conjunction with Area Maritime Security (AMS) Committees in each AOR.

The actions described below assist the responsible COTP and are presented in three categories: public safety/security, security of the MTS, and safe/secure restoration of maritime commerce operations.

Recovery operations at the security incident site will incorporate considerations to protect the economy of the United States as discussed earlier. The COTP at the incident site must evaluate the cumulative restrictive effects of terrorist activities and balance them with response management activities. The projected impact and duration of these restrictions should be reported to the HSOC as soon as possible to aid federal decision makers regarding their responsibilities for the restoration of maritime commerce capacity and capabilities.

If the incident restricts maritime commerce at the incident site, the COTP must consider options to continue limited commerce activities to mitigate effects on the economy. All decisions to restrict or allow maritime commerce activities must be determined using threat-based, consequence-driven risk-management protocols. Once the threat has been eliminated or controlled, recovery operations should begin as soon as possible. Rapid recovery of the incident site's ability to participate in commerce and reintegrate into MTS operations is essential to mitigating the debilitating effects upon the U.S. economy.

The COTP/FMSC should consider establishing a Unified Command using the principles contained in the National Incident Management System (NIMS). The Unified Command (UC) will provide needed SMEs and mobilize appropriate federal, state, local and tribal governments and private sector organizations to support larger scale MTS recovery operations. It is recommended that the UC Operations and Planning Sections include a <u>Recovery Branch</u>, separate from the Response Branch, to facilitate concurrent recovery and response activities. Representatives from other transportation sectors, such as highway and rail, and the private sector should be included in the UC as appropriate. *Potential Recovery Branch members should be identified in advance and be provided training in the principles of NIMS.*

A national TSI site response and recovery considerations

To guide COTP/FMSCs in planning both response and recovery activities in AMS Plans, COTP/FMSCs use Coast Guard Navigation and Vessel Inspection Circular (NVIC) instructions and planning elements in 33 CFR 103, which are limited in scope. There is a need for additional guidance to develop further recovery aspects of AMS Plans. This guidance will be found in the NMSP. The information in this section of the MIRP is being recommended for use in developing AMS Plans. (See Next Steps/ Recommendations Section). COTP/FMSCs should consider the following topics, as well as port stakeholders' continuity of operations plans, in planning for both response and recovery:

<u>Planning for Response and Recovery</u>

- Major transportation routes needed for emergency services, including evacuation tunnels, bridges, and key waterways
- Main shipping channels critical for homeland security and homeland defense operations

- Anchorage capacity—evaluate capacity and identify a quarantine/isolation anchorage
- Barge fleet facilities—evaluate capacity and identify a quarantine/isolation area
- Port areas and channels critical for military traffic or out-loads
- Secondary bridges and tunnels
- Main shipping channels critical to major commercial operations;
- Secondary commercial waterways
- Environmental protection/response
- Manpower issues: coordinate with federal, state, and local government agencies;
- Public/recreational waterways
- Key infrastructure according to its importance in maintaining continuity of operations at each port and the procedures for restoring maritime transportation infrastructure integrity

Response Activities

- Conduct Safety of Life and Health/ Search and Rescue
- Set appropriate MARSEC and Force Protection levels
- Take risk mitigation measures IAW Operation Neptune Shield
- Establish Security Zones
- Coordinate with key agencies and marine stakeholders
- Assess damage
- Survey channels and waterways
- Remove debris
- Conduct dredging and/or salvage operations

Recovery Considerations

Eliminate/control threat.

- Provide for public safety
- Abate hazards

Establish site security: Security decisions should be soundly based on the risk management principles outlined in Appendix B.

- Establish MARSEC and Force Protection Condition
- Ensure adequate numbers of escort vessels are available
- Confirm enforcement of facility and vessel security plans
- Establish and enforce security zones
- Determine vessel movement restrictions (e.g., recreational boating)

Assess and restore functionality to essential MTS infrastructure.

- Survey channels and waterways
    - Dredging and salvage operations, as appropriate
    - Remove debris
- Verify or reposition Aids to Navigation

- Verify pier conditions
  - Pier equipment
  - Storage areas
  - Avenues for intermodal connections
- Verify pipeline integrity, as appropriate
- In consultation with industry (especially importers), evaluate which vessels awaiting inbound transit could divert cargo to another port.

Establish passenger and cargo priorities.

- National priorities
- Regional priorities
- Local priorities: The COTP may establish a stakeholder team to analyze vessel specific information and needs.
  - Identify and consider vessels awaiting inbound transit (this is not a prioritization scheme, but a planning consideration).
    - Winter (specific to the cold weather ports):
      Vessels carrying fuel oil (specific to cold weather ports);
      Vessels carrying gas and diesel;
      Vessels with perishable cargo;
      Vessels with assembly line components; and
      Other vessels (based on other factors evaluated by the COTP/FMSC).
    - Summer:
      Vessels carrying gas and diesel;
      Vessels with perishable cargo;
      Vessels with assembly line components; and
      Other vessels (based on other priorities evaluated by the COTP/FMSC).

Queue Management.

- In cooperation with CBP, establish screening and inspection criteria for inbound passengers and cargo. CBP programs are described in this plan's National-Regional Coordination and Procedures;
- Identify and consider vessels currently in the port for outbound transit;
  - Reopen anchorages on a limited basis for vessels requiring service prior to inbound transit;
  - Allow for limited refueling, lightering, and bunkering operations;
  - Identify and stage vessels of low interest;
- Identify and stage vessels requiring inspection;
- Establish/verify anchorages/barge fleet facilities;
- Establish isolation/quarantine anchorage; and
- Confirm adequate numbers of escort vessels are available.

Work Force Issues.

- Organized labor
- Pilots, tug and barge operators

- Industry specific (i.e. brokers)
- Boarding teams
- Security forces
- CBP inspection teams

Intermodal connections

- Facilities' status
- Capacities and capabilities
- Equipment
- Personnel

Re-Integration into the Maritime Transportation System (MTS)

USCG COTPs have lead responsibility for determining re-opening of port facilities and movement of vessels following an emergency affecting a port community. Using port decision criteria and considerations from the applicable Area Maritime Security Plan(s) as a starting point, the COTP will work with other members of the private sector and the port community to refine and apply them to the specific incident. Participants in the decision-making process may include the U.S. Coast Guard, local Port Authority, Pilot's Association, facility representatives, and Marine Exchange or Mariner's Advisory Committees as well as certain members of the AMS Committee and OPA 90 Area Committee as determined appropriate by the COTP. While the maritime community will inform and advise the COTP on re-opening considerations and priorities, the COTP retains final decision authority for planning and executing port re-opening priorities.

If a port community is affected by a national TSI that has an appointed Primary Federal Official (PFO), the COTP will inform the PFO of the plans for port re-opening and vessel traffic movement control. In the event of significant national or regional needs, the IIMG or the PFO may establish prioritization criteria to assist affected COTPs in the planning of port re-opening prioritizations and/or reserve/surge operations at other ports.

V. MARITIME INFRASTRUCTURE RECOVERY PLAN EXERCISE PROGRAM

The Maritime Infrastructure Recovery Plan (MIRP) is one of a number of interconnected plans that supports the nation's goal of optimizing preparedness, prevention, response, and recovery from Incidents of National Significance or a national TSI.

To maintain preparedness and continuous improvement, the MIRP is subject to periodic evaluation along with the other plans. The primary means to evaluate the effectiveness of various plans is to participate in periodic exercises (e.g., table-top exercises (TTX) and field training exercises (FTX)).

The MIRP Exercise Program reaches across the spectrum of the maritime community and may involve participation of federal, state, and local government and private sector/maritime industry stakeholders. The exercise program aligns with various plans and programs, including:

- National Response Plan (NRP);
- National Maritime Security Plan's National Maritime Exercise Program; and
- Top Official (TOPOFF) Program.

SCOPE

The MIRP Exercise Program lays the foundation to validate the ability of the maritime community to effectively plan, respond (prevent and protect), and recover from Incidents of National Significance or a national TSI. Particular to recovery, the program conducts the following:

- Execute and attain MARSEC level changes during the exercise.
- Implement risk reduction and mitigation strategies.
- Implement linkages with federal, state, port and local recovery plans.
- Identify, prioritize, and implement short- and long-term infrastructure recovery strategies.

OBJECTIVE

One objective of the MIRP Exercise Program is to assess the MIRP's adequacy to support federal, state, local government, and private sector efforts to recover from Incidents of National Significance or a national TSI and evaluate the following:

- Roles, responsibilities, and authorities for recovery management.
- Overall risk mitigation strategies.
- Procedures and tools for recovery and reconstitution of the Maritime Transportation Systems (MTS).

The MIRP Exercise Program is described further in the National Maritime Security Plan (NMSP). The program recognizes practicable limits to the number and scale of exercises that can be conducted effectively. The federal agencies responsible for sustaining the MIRP and the NMSP will work closely with key stakeholders to ensure that the overarching MIRP Exercise Program is compatible with, and to the extent practical, integrated into other existing national and local port area exercise programs.

It is anticipated that full exercise of the MIRP will take place in each of the five broad geographic areas once every ten years. Elements of the NMSP/MIRP will be exercised in every port area around the country at least once every 3 years as part of the AMS Plan exercises held at the port level. Additionally, various aspects of recovery are included in exercise event scenarios in other types of exercises more frequently held. Most recently, some aspects of maritime infrastructure recovery were evaluated in TOPOFF 2005.

Refer to the NMSP National Maritime Exercise Program for further information about the MIRP Exercise Program and its protocol.

VI. NEXT STEPS/RECOMMENDATIONS

Due to the accelerated timeline established for the development of HSPD-13 plans, the Maritime Infrastructure Recovery Plan (MIRP) could not fully address the planning Objectives as originally laid out. Additionally, a number of issues of concern have been identified which, although not immediately falling under the direct purview of the MIRP, warrant further evaluation with regard to efficacy and appropriateness for implementation.

- **Issue #1:** The recovery decision-making process must be informed from its very outset by <u>risk management/analysis</u> expertise to avoid unnecessary imposition of constraints on the Maritime Transportation System (MTS).

  Recommendation: Homeland Security Operations Center (HSOC) should have permanently assigned, appropriately trained risk-management personnel to support the Inter-agency Incident Management Group's (IIMG) Subject Matter Experts (SME) in formulation of recommended courses of action pertaining to recovery and restoration of cargo flow.

- **Issue #2:** Port <u>cargo-handling capacity</u> information at both the national and individual port levels is not readily available for use in deliberations regarding recovery of the Maritime Transportation System (MTS) following a national TSI.

  Recommendations:
  - Establish a uniform measurement standard for port cargo-handling capacity for individual ports as well as for capacity of the MTS.
  - Establish the requirement for individual port facility operators to provide port cargo-handling information to the Federal Maritime Security Coordinator (FMSC).
  - Create a baseline for port cargo-handling capacity.
  - Maintain data in a form that can be used to support recovery efforts.
  - Create incentives to establish sufficient cargo-handling capacity to satisfy the requirements for the worst-case scenario.

- **Issue #3:** Recovery decision makers are not aware of the availability of <u>international port cargo-handling capacity</u> for diversion and facilitation of U.S.-bound cargo and passengers.

  Recommendations:
  - Initiate foreign port cargo-handling capacity studies.
  - Develop international agreements designed to ease enforcement of cargo clearance requirements for the purpose of facilitating redistribution of cargo through Canada and Central America following a national TSI.

- **Issue #4**: There is an absence of an agreed upon maritime sector <u>communications network</u> which facilitates information sharing between government and the private sector marine industry stakeholders.

  Recommendations:
  - o Expand access to and capabilities of the web-based Homeland Security Information Network (HSIN) to facilitate sharing of information pertaining to recovery activities with the private sector.
  - o To facilitate sharing of pertinent information, encourage members of the maritime commerce community to file business continuity plans (or relevant information from them) with the NICC's Protected Critical Infrastructure Information (PCII) Program. Continuity plans should be accessible by multiple criteria, i.e. business name, region, type conveyance.
  - o Widely publicize the Transportation Sector Coordinating Council (SCC) membership and procedures for sharing information with government..

- **Issue #5**: <u>FMSC Area Maritime Security (AMS) Plans</u> required under the provisions of 33CFR 103 do not adequately and uniformly address the critical MTS recovery management planning elements.

  Recommendation: Establish requirements for AMS Plans to implement MIRP recovery management procedures informed by port stakeholders' continuity of operations plans.

- **Issue #6**: Information regarding the status of the <u>salvage capability</u> specific to national and regional capacity is poorly understood. Currently, recovery management at the national level does not include salvage expertise in critical decision making to recover the MTS.

  Recommendations:
  - o Include a marine salvage expert as part of the cadre of IIMG SMEs assembled in response to a national TSI.
  - o * Include a representative of the professional marine salvage community as a designated member of the National Maritime Security Advisory Council (NMSAC).
  - o * Establish an inventory of salvage and firefighting assets maintained by the U.S. Navy Supervisor Salvage (SupSal) in consultation with the U.S. Coast Guard.
  - o * Conduct a thorough gap analysis, comparing available assets to those assets needed to respond effectively to a range of potential terrorist activities. The analysis should consider all critical salvage response measures including: rescue towing; harbor and channel clearing; emergency dredging; search and recovery; patching and re-floating of

---

*Recommendations taken from the August 2003 Transportation Research Board Marine Salvage Response Capability Workshop

vessels; and maritime firefighting. The adequacy of anticipated response times on a regional basis should be included along with identification of optimal geographic locations for the pre-staging of salvage equipment.

- **Issue # 7:** Private Sector expertise is not uniformly available to senior decision makers at the national and regional levels when developing strategies for dealing with the restoration of passenger and cargo flow and recovery of maritime infrastructure in response to an INS.

  Recommendation: The Policy Directorate Office of the Private Sector should utilize the National Maritime Security Advisory Committee (NMSAC) to identify maritime SMEs to participate in the IIMG. SMEs are key to further identifying members of the private sector who are essential to implementing the National and Regional Recovery Management Procedures recommended in the MIRP.

Appendix A: Area Maritime Security (AMS) Planning (Stakeholders)

Organization of Area Maritime Security (AMS) Committees

The local membership and organization of the Area Maritime Security (AMS) Committees will take into account all aspects of the MTS in each port area and its adjacent waterways and coastal areas. The AMS Committees are comprised of federal, state, and local agencies, law enforcement and security agencies, and port stakeholders. Representatives for each aspect of the MTS and those charged with its regulation or enforcement should be encouraged to participate.

AMS Committee membership could include, but is not limited to, representatives from the following agencies and organizations:

<u>Federal Agencies:</u>

- U.S. Coast Guard (e.g., Groups, Air Stations, Small Boat Stations, VTS, MSSTs, Auxiliaries);
- Department of Defense (DoD);
- Department of State (DOS);
- Nuclear Regulatory Commission (NRC);
- U.S. Northern Command (USNORTHCOM);
- U.S. Pacific Command (USPACOM);
- U.S. Department of Agriculture (USDA);
- Environmental Protection Agency (EPA);
- Occupational Safety and Health Agency (OSHA);
- United States Attorney;
- Federal Bureau of Investigation;
- Federal Emergency Management Agency (FEMA);
- Bureau of Customs and Border Protection (BCBP);
- Bureau of Immigration and Customs Enforcement (BICE);
- Transportation Security Administration (TSA);
- Army Corps of Engineers (USACE);
- U.S. Transportation Command (USTRANSCOM);
- Military Sealift Command (MSC);
- Military Surface Deployment and Distribution Command (SDDC);
- Animal and Plant Health Inspection Service (APHIS);
- Maritime Administration (MARAD);
- Federal Railway Administration (FRA);
- Federal Highway Administration (FHWA);
- Pipeline and Hazardous Materials Safety Administration;

- Federal Transit Administration (FTA); and
- Other government representatives, where appropriate.

State and Local agencies:

- National Guard;
- Marine Police;
- Port Authority Police and/or security forces;
- Fire Departments;
- Civil Defense;
- City Government officials;
- Transportation agencies;
- Fish and Wildlife marine units;
- Health agencies;
- Occupational safety agencies;
- Terminal/facility security forces;
- Pilot associations;
- Other State, local and City Government representatives;
- State Department of Natural or Environmental Resources marine units;
- Other environmental agencies;
- Regional development agencies/metropolitan planning organizations; and
- Tribal authorities and tribal organizations.

Industry related organizations:

- Facility owners/operators;
- Terminal owners/operators;
- Trade organizations;
- Recreational boating organizations (yacht clubs, rowing clubs);
- Railroad companies;
- Trucking companies;
- Shipyards;
- Tow-boat operators;
- Marine exchanges;
- Vessel operators;
- Organized labor;
- Commercial fishing industry;
- Waterborne vendors & service providers (harbor tugs, launch services, line handlers, small ferry operators, water taxis); and
- Other facilities within the port having waterside access (refineries, chemical plants, power plants, etc.).

APPENDIX B: RISK MANAGEMENT PRINCIPLES

RISK MANAGEMENT PRINCIPLES

Risk management is a systematic process to analyze the threats, vulnerabilities, and consequences (or relative importance) of assets in a program to better support key decisions, linking resources and program results. Risk management is used by many organizations in both government and the private sector. In recent years, we have consistently advocated the use of a risk management approach to help implement and assess responses to various national security and terrorism issues. Without a risk management approach that provides insights about the present threat, consequences and vulnerabilities, as well as the organizational and technical requirements necessary to achieve specified goals and objectives, there is little assurance that MTS recovery strategies will be prioritized and properly focused. Risk management helps to more effectively and efficiently prepare defenses against future post-national TSI acts of terrorism and unnecessary disruptions to the flow of cargo and maintenance of overall equilibrium within the MTS. Key elements of a risk management approach are listed below:

- Threat assessment: A threat assessment identifies adverse events that can affect an entity, and may be present at the global, national, or local level. The threat assessment considers the intent of the terrorist agent, capability of the terrorist agents to implement the action, the overall simplicity of the attack;
- Consequence assessment: A consequence assessment identifies and evaluates the importance of an asset based on the potential for loss of life, economic impact, adverse impact on the environment, strategic military considerations and national iconic value;
- Vulnerability assessment: A vulnerability assessment identifies weaknesses in physical structures, personnel protection systems, processes, general availability of the target or other areas that may be exploited by terrorists;
- Risk assessment: A risk assessment qualitatively and/or quantitatively determines the likelihood of an adverse event occurring and the severity, or impact, of its consequences;
- Risk characterization: Risk characterization involves designating risk on a scale, for example, low, medium, or high. Risk characterization forms the basis for deciding which actions are best suited to mitigate risk;
- Mitigation evaluation: Mitigation evaluation is the identification of mitigating alternatives to assess the effectiveness of the alternatives. The alternatives should be evaluated for their likely effect on the risk and their cost;
- Mitigation selection: Mitigation selection involves a management decision on which mitigation alternatives should be implemented. Selection among alternatives should be based on pre-considered criteria;
- Systems approach: An integrated systems approach to risk management encompasses taking action in all organizational areas, including personnel, processes, technology, infrastructure, and governance; and

- Monitoring and evaluation: Monitoring and evaluation is a continuous repetitive assessment process to keep risk management current and relevant.

APPENDIX C: ACRONYMS

AMS - Area Maritime Security

AOR - Area of Responsibility

APIS – Advance Passenger Information System

ATS – Automated Targeting System

ATSA - Aviation and Transportation Security Act

CBP - Customs and Border Protection

CI - Critical Infrastructure

COA - Courses of Action

COCOM – Combatant Commander

COP - Common Operating Picture

COTP - Captain of the Port

CSI - Container Security Initiative

C-TPAT – Customs-Trade Partnership Against Terrorism

DHS - Department of Homeland Security

DOC - Department of Commerce

DoD - Department of Defense

DOE - Department of Energy

DOI - Department of Interior

DOJ - Department of Justice

DOS - Department of State

DOT - Department of Transportation

DPA - Defense Production Act

DSCA - Defense Support of Civil Authorities

EOC - Emergency Operations Center

EPA - Environmental Protection Agency

EPR - Emergency Preparedness and Response

ESFs - Emergency Support Functions

FBI - Federal Bureau of Investigation

FCO - Federal Coordination Officer

FEMA - Federal Emergency Management Agency

FHWA - Federal Highway Administration

FMSC - Federal Maritime Security Coordinator

FRA - Federal Railroad Administration

FTX - Field Training Exercises

GAR - Governor's Authorized Representative

HSAS - Homeland Security Alert System

HSC - Homeland Security Council

HSOC - Homeland Security Operations Center

HSPD - Homeland Security Presidential Directive

I&A – Office of Intelligence and Analysis

ICS - Incident Command System

ICE - U.S. Immigration and Customs Enforcement

ICP - Incident Command Post

IIMG - Interagency Incident Management Group

IMO - International Maritime Organization

INS - Incident of National Significance

IO - Bureau of International Organization Affairs

IP – Infrastructure Protection

ISAC - Information Sharing and Analysis Center

ISPS - International Ship and Port Facility Security

JFO - Joint Field Office

JTTF - Joint Terrorism Task Forces

KA - Key Asset

LFA - Lead Federal Agency

MARAD - Maritime Administration

MARSEC - Maritime Security

MCI - Maritime Critical Infrastructure

MIRP - Maritime Infrastructure Recovery Plan

MOL - Military Out Load

MOTR - Maritime Operation Threat Response

MOU - Memorandum of Understanding

MSP - Maritime Security Plans

MSWG - Maritime Security Work Group

MTS - Maritime Transportation System

MTSA - Maritime Transportation Security Act

NGO - Non-Governmental Organization

NICC - National Infrastructure Coordination Center

NIMS - National Incident Management System

NIPP - National Infrastructure Protection Plan

NJTTF - National Joint Terrorism Task Force

NMSAC - National Maritime Security Advisory Committees

NMSP - National Maritime Security Plan

MSC - Military Sealift Command

NOA - Notice of Arrival

NOAA - National Oceanic and Atmospheric Administration

NRCC - National Response and Coordination Center

NRP - National Response Plan

NSC - National Security Council

NSMS - National Strategy for Maritime Security

NSSE - National Special Security Events

NTC - National Targeting Center

National TSI - National Transportation Security Incident

NVIC - Navigation and Vessel Inspection Circular

OES - Office of Oceans and International Environment and Scientific Affairs

OGA - Other Governmental Agencies

OIA - Office of the Assistant Secretary for Information Analysis

PCC - Policy Coordination Committees

PCII – Protected Critical Infrastructure Information

PFO – Principal Federal Official

S/CT - Office of the Coordinator for Counterterrorism

SAC - Special Agent In Charge

SCC - Sector Coordinating Council

SCO - State Coordinating Officer

SDDC - Military Surface Deployment and Distribution Command

SECDOT - Secretary of Transportation

SFLEO - Senior Federal Law Enforcement Official

SFO - Senior Federal Officials

SIOC - Strategic Information Operations Center

SLSDC - St. Lawrence Seaway Development Corporation

SMEs - Subject Matter Experts

SSP - Sector Specific Plans

SSR - Sector Specific Responsibility

TOPOFF - Top Official

TSA - Transportation Security Administration

SCC - Sector Coordinating Council

TSI - Transportation Security Incident

TSOP - Transportation Security Operations Plans

TSSP - Transportation Sector Specific Plan

TTX – Table-Top Exercise

TWIC - Transportation Worker ID Credential

UCS - Unified Command Structure

UN - United Nations

USACE - U.S. Army Corps of Engineers

USCG - U.S. Coast Guard

USTRANSCOM - US Transportation Command